A Song for Lovers

S. Craig Glickman

Including a new paraphrase and a new
translation of The Song of Solomon

InterVarsity Press
Downers Grove
Illinois 60515

InterVarsity Press is the book-publishing division of Inter-Varsity Christian Fellowship, a student movement active on campus at hundreds of universities, colleges and schools of nursing. For information about local and regional activities, write IVCF, 233 Langdon St., Madison, WI 53703.

Distributed in Canada through InterVarsity Press, 1875 Leslie St., Unit 10, Don Mills, Ontario M3B 2M5, Canada.

Acknowledgment is made for permission to reprint a portion from "Love's As Warm As Tears" in Poems by C. S. Lewis, copyright © by the Executors of the Estate of C. S. Lewis. Reprinted by permission of Harcourt Brace Jovanovich, Inc., New York, Wm. Collins Sons & Co. Ltd., Glasgow, and the Trustees of the Estate of C. S. Lewis.

Cover illustration: Joe DeVelasco

ISBN 0-87784-768-1
Library of Congress Catalog Card Number: 75-21454

Printed in the United States of America

22	21	20	19	18	17	16	15	14	13	12	11	10	9	8	7
96	95	94	93	92	91	90	89	88	87	86	85	84	83	82	

*I gratefully dedicate this book to
Dr. Bruce Waltke,
who taught me to interpret the Old Testament
Mr. Jackie Deere,
who long studied this song with me
and The Young Life family
from White High School,
whose bright faces prompted the
writing of this book*

CONTENTS

FOREWORD

Back in Sunday school, when I first riveted the books of the Old Testament in my memory, I routinely learned the six books of poetry: Job, Psalms, Proverbs, Ecclesiastes, Song of Solomon and Lamentations. The first three were familiar because preachers talked about them in their sermons. The other three were just names.

Eventually I managed to attach Lamentations to the weeping prophet, Jeremiah, and to peg Ecclesiastes as a look at life from man's viewpoint. But what to do with Solomon's Song? Most writers simply called it a highly symbolic poem depicting marital love.

Indeed, some scholars seem to balk at accepting a literal interpretation of it. Admittedly, to say that Scripture means exactly what it says may sometimes lead us into interpretive briar patches. We may be left badly scratched, admitting that we don't understand. We can't fit the ideas together logically—or in the case of the Song of Solomon—delicately.

Nevertheless, the author of A Song for Lovers has dared to accept the challenge of a literal interpretation of Solomon's poetic ode to love and to present it, unabashed, as the Bible does, as a part of normal life.

Sensuous love with erotic overtones is God's intent for the marriage relationship. The distortion of that relationship has no doubt abased this dimension of life, but that does not justify placing such experience —or Scripture's Song about it—into the inactive file of living.

The Song of Songs overflows with poetic imagery. But love in literature has always been best expressed that way, and the richly poetic mind of a millennium before Christ was particularly geared to this avenue of communication. The imagery is sometimes notoriously difficult, but its explanation becomes the key to unlocking the true meaning of Solomon's Canticles. Here is a noble and worthy effort, a refreshing and honest look into a chest of jewels whose lid has been clamped tight for so long.

Any rare and exotic work of art is best appreciated with the help of a knowledgeable guide. I invite the reader to step with the author into this immortal Song and hear God himself speak on the subject of human love at its highest aesthetic level.

Howard G. Hendricks
Professor of Christian Education
Dallas Theological Seminary

1

A Night to Remember

Did my heart
e'er love till now?
Forswear it, sight.
For I ne'er saw
true beauty till this night.
William Shakespeare,
Romeo and Juliet

ONE

No artist could have fashioned two people better suited for one another. He was the king of their great nation; she, his chosen bride. Spring had seen their love blossom like the flowers in the palace gardens. Their love had been the talk of the court. It was destined to be a song for the world. For their romance was a romance for all seasons, indeed, for all centuries. And, in fact, so ideal was their love that the song about them was chosen as one of the books of sacred Scripture. It became the only one of the entire collection devoted exclusively to courtship and marriage.

It was now the night their courtship would end and their marriage begin. The wedding guests had gone. The evening had come. The clamor and laughter had ceased. The endless chatter scarcely heard throughout the day had echoed softly to this silence. Yet it was an eloquent silence, the silence of anticipation of love fulfilled. All the excitement and fervor of their courtship had come to this moment... of shy and peaceful silence. He was the first to speak. And when he spoke he could not but praise the loveliness of his bride.

Compliment or Ridicule?

"Your hair is like a flock of goats which descend from Mount Gilead." What in the world does the king mean by this? Is he blowing the whole romance by insulting his bride on their wedding night? Let's face it. Few girls today would like to hear anyone say that about their hair. I know for a fact.

One afternoon I was flying back from Colorado with my good friend Guy Owen, and we had been discussing the obscurity of the figures of speech in this song. Later I was trying to engage the stewardess in conversation when Guy (with nothing to lose since he was already married) motioned to the stewardess and said, "You know, Miss, your hair looks like a flock of goats which descend from Mount Gilead." She walked off and said nothing to us the rest of the flight. It just didn't sound exactly like a compliment and he knew it wouldn't. What a way to prove a point!

Nevertheless, the king said the very same words to his bride on their wedding night. How can we explain this? The explanation must be found in the kind of figures of speech he was using as he praised his bride. It is obvious they are metaphors. But they are a special kind of metaphor which gain much of their meaning from the emotional feelings one associates with them.

For example, later in his praise, the king will tell his bride, "Your two breasts are like two fawns, twins of a gazelle." He does not mean that her breasts look like two fawns—complete with four legs, two ears and a tail. It is ridiculous to think so. Almost every reader recognizes that the emotional associations with the fawn help reveal the meaning of this figure of speech.

A baby deer is soft and gentle, and everyone seeing these little deer long to pet them and play with them. Thus, when the king compares her breasts to two fawns, he is really saying that he longs to caress her soft and tender breasts.

We need to recognize this principle of interpretation when we read the other compliments on their wedding night too. The emotional associations of the metaphor are a clue to its overall meaning.

So when we hear him say that her hair is like a flock of goats descending from Mount Gilead, we need to remember the emotional associations with such a scene. It is perhaps the end of a long day, so the goats are descending from the mountain. Across the valley is seen an entire flock moving together down the mountain. The individual members of the flock blend in to form a dark stream flowing smoothly to the valley. The peacefulness of the evening and the flowing movement of the flock tell us that the long flowing hair of the bride is very attractive, almost hypnotic to the king. And elsewhere in the song, this interpretation is confirmed because the king tells us that he is held captive by her hair. This pictures the king playfully entangled and bound by her hair which was so attractive to him.

Love's Prelude

Frequently when someone experiences great beauty, he finds that ordinary words are inadequate for expression. He gropes for poetry that may capture something of the beauty he sees. The king had this experience on his wedding night. With his bride before him, he searches for the perfect words of praise for her. Seven verses of the song recount these praises of his bride on their wedding night. When at last the king was alone with his bride, his first words were these words of praise:

4:1   *Behold, you are beautiful, my darling; behold,*
        you are beautiful.
     Your eyes are doves from behind your veil.
     Your hair is like a flock of goats which descend
        from Mount Gilead.

  2   *Your teeth are like a flock of newly shorn sheep*
        which have come up from the washing,

all of which are paired,
and not one of them is alone.

3   *Like a scarlet thread are your lips,*
and your mouth is lovely.
Your temples are like a slice of a pomegranate
behind your veil.

4   *Like the tower of David is your neck, built for warfare—*
a thousand shields hang upon it,
all the shields of the mighty men.

5   *Your two breasts are like two fawns, twins of a gazelle,*
which feed among the lilies.

6   *Until the day breathes and the shadows flee,*
I will go my way to the mountain of myrrh
and hill of frankincense.

7   *You are altogether fair, my love, and there is*
no blemish in you.

When he praises her eyes like doves, he seems to mean that her eyes were bright and alert, soft and innocent. Very interestingly, when she will later describe him, the only identical praise she returns is with respect to his eyes. They, too, were like doves. They must have looked at life and love the same way.

Next he praises her lovely hair, and we have already observed that this compliment praises the long, flowing nature of her hair and the captivating effect it has on him.

Numerous readers have stumbled over his praise of her teeth. When he compares them to sheep, does he mean they are like wool? No, that is not likely. It is fairly apparent that he praises the evenness and completeness of her teeth when he says they are like sheep, "all of which are paired, and not one of them is alone." And their glistening whiteness, so lovely when she smiles, is praised when he adds, "which have come up from the washing." But a deeper meaning can also be given to this phrase. Seeing these little animals newly shorn come scurrying up out of the water must surely have been an amusing sight. Who does not smile, for example, at playful dogs trying to get dry after a bath? Just as these little lambs cause him to smile, her smile causes him to smile in return.

Next he compliments her lips like a scarlet thread. Some readers actually have thought that she must have had very thin lips. But it is doubtful that this is the meaning. Connoisseurs of such things have noticed that the delicate outline of a girl's features frequently determines her beauty, especially with respect to her lips. It is this delicate form he praises. With a scarlet thread an artist could perfectly shape a woman's lips. For example, the king could not say "Like a scarlet rope are your lips." Trying to shape lips with a rope would produce a blob! But the lips of his bride were delicately beautiful.

Her temples were like a pomegranate. Probably the red color of this fruit and perhaps its association in the ancient world with romance determine the meaning of this compliment. Her "temples" (which probably includes her cheeks) were healthy and flushed with excitement and beauty.

The king was not interested only in the physical beauty of his bride, however. He deeply appreciated her character and integrity too. Hence, he says to her, "Like the tower of David is your neck." In the ancient world, especially, the position of the neck was believed to reflect character. The neck bent over was a picture of humiliation. The "stiff-necked" person was stubborn. What does it mean that her neck was reminiscent of the tower of David?

This does not mean she looked like a giraffe (as some have surmised)! One must remember that the feelings associated with the metaphor are the key to its meaning. The tower of David was a military fortress of the nation. The country depended upon the faithfulness and integrity of that fortress. And it must have been very reassuring to look upon that awesome stronghold, displaying as it did all the shields of war. The people had a healthy respect for it. Therefore, when the king likens the neck of his bride to the fortress, he is paying her a great compliment. The way she carries herself reflects an integrity and character that breeds a healthy respect from all who see her.

Next the king praises the lovely and gentle breasts of his bride. "Your two breasts are like two fawns, twins of a gazelle, which feed among the lilies." He longed to caress them as one would caress the fawns, and with that he concludes his praise.

So far the king has altogether praised seven different aspects of his bride's beauty. In their culture seven was the number of perfection. So even in the number of compliments he gives, the king tells his bride how perfect she is for him. Not unexpectedly, then, he summarizes his praise by declaring to her that she is altogether beautiful and that there is no blemish in her. She is flawless to him.

No question that the king has a healthy appreciation for the outer beauty as well as the inner beauty of his bride. How could some people have gained the impression that the Scripture does not endorse such physical beauty?

Yet the Scripture also endorses their lovemaking. Just before the summary of praise in 4:7, the king declares, "Until the day breathes and the shadows flee, I will go my way to the mountain of myrrh and hill of frankincense." This is really an answer to a request made by his bride during courtship. Once she had asked of him, "Until the day breathes and the shadows flee, turn, my beloved, and be like a gazelle or a young stag on the mountains of separation" (2:17).

The new day would breathe and the shadows of darkness flee at daybreak. The phrase, "mountains of separation," is likely her very delicate and restrained reference to her breasts. With propriety, then, she asks for that which cannot be given until their wedding night—the full expression of their love all through the night.

But did you notice the slight alteration the king has made in answering his bride's former request. She had referred to her breasts merely as the "mountains of separation." Yet to the king they were not as ordinary as that. They were not simply mountains separated. They were mountains of myrrh and frankincense—fragrant, refreshing and intoxicating as the best perfume.

Now that the wedding night has come, it is perfume which he can and will enjoy. He will fulfill her request and hence declare that until the light of dawn breaks they will give their love to one another. How sensitive it was of the king to eloquently praise his bride on their wedding night. Even the loveliest girl might feel insecure on this occasion. Yet as always he was sensitive to her and careful to make her secure in his love.

Make the World Go Away

Having praised his bride, the king calls her thoughts from afar.

4:8 *With me from Lebanon, O bride, with me from Lebanon come.*
Journey from the peak of Amana,
 from the peak of Senir and Hermon,
 from the dens of lions and the mountains of leopards.

The request by the king to his bride that she come from Lebanon, from the peak of Amana and the peak of Senir and Hermon, has puzzled some readers. In Lebanon in the north of their country were these mountain peaks. Why does he ask her to come from them? One reader jokingly suggested that Hermon was the name of an old boyfriend, and so the king is asking that she forget about Hermon and bring her thoughts to himself. But most realize that Hermon is the name of a mountain in the north, not an old boyfriend.

But is the king really asking that she come from the dens of lions and the mountains of leopards? Would she ever have lived in such an unlikely place? Probably not, and in light of this being their wedding night we can be sure that his request has a deeper meaning.

The dens of lions and the mountains of leopards were fearful places to the north, perhaps near her homeland. In asking her to come from such fearful places, he is really asking her to bring her thoughts completely to him and leave her fears behind and perhaps to leave the lingering thoughts of home behind as well. In the same way a fearful traveler would journey from the dark and threatening mountains to the safety of the valley below, so he wished her to leave her fear and anxiety about the new life of marriage and simply come to him.

It is very significant that he makes this reassuring request just before they begin to give each other the caresses of love because in the gentle kisses and caresses that follow they actually bring their thoughts completely to one another. He helps her fulfill the request he gave. The request, therefore, gives us at least one purpose for the lovemaking that precedes the consummation of their marriage. It is designed to focus totally one lover's thoughts upon the other. Most people realize that this "foreplay" is designed to prepare the body physically for intercourse, but few emphasize that it equally serves to prepare the heart emotionally for genuine giving.

One person cannot give with his whole heart while half of his heart is distracted by all the events of a busy day, especially the hustle and bustle of the wedding day. One purpose of petting, then, is to enable both lovers to forget everything else and look only at the other. In so doing they prepare themselves both physically and emotionally for the sincerest giving.

So by his request the king reveals that he was anxious not only to fulfill his own desires. He realized that his new bride might be fearful and, like most women, more slowly aroused than a man. Yet he wanted to bring her patiently to the fullest experience that was possible for their wedding night. So he calls her from her fears to his arms.

A Taste of Honey

Marriage counselors have frequently noted that a common complaint among women, is the brief and perfunctory time of lovemaking they receive from their husbands. The husband seems to be not so much interested in expressing and enjoying the delights of love as he is in satisfying his own desires. But the king is much in love, so he tenderly gives love to his new bride.

4:9   *You have made my heart beat fast, my sister, my bride.*
You have made my heart beat fast
   with one glance of your eyes,
   with one jewel of your necklace.

10   *How beautiful are your caresses, my sister, my bride.*
How much better are your caresses than wine
   and the fragrance of your perfumes than any spice.

11   *Your lips, (my) bride, drip honey;*
Honey and milk are under your tongue,
   and the fragrance of your garments is like
     the fragrance of Lebanon.

Just to look at her eyes was enough to excite him. He had looked forward to this night for a long time. At last she would become his wife. By the way, that is the reason he calls her his sister. In their culture "sister" was an affectionate term for one's wife.

She's not passive either. Notice he tells her that her caresses were beautiful, better than wine. And her kisses were remarkable too. No doubt some historians of romance are under the illusion that a certain kind of kissing originated in France in recent centuries. This song, however, was written long before that. And way back then the king tells his bride that honey and milk are under her tongue. But this expression may tell us more than that French kissing was around long before the French.

We might remember that the richness of the land God promised his people was frequently described as the land of milk and honey.

These spoke of the great richness and blessings of the land. Of course, the king was aware of this description because it was now his land. Perhaps, just perhaps, he is telling his bride that all the blessing and the happiness the nation was to find in its land he had found in her arms. That was quite a compliment. But also in saying this, he recognized that she, like the land, was a wonderful gift from God.

One Hand, One Heart

Many modern people in reaction against prudish hypocrisy demand that sex be spoken of frankly and openly. But often they succeed only in being crude or "scientific" and thus leave no room for the beauty of the sacredness of the sexual expression of love. Thankfully, the couple of our song knew otherwise. Their love is consummated in one of the shyest and most delicate of love scenes in world literature.

4:12   *A garden locked is my sister, (my) bride.*
        A spring locked, a fountain sealed.

13   *Your shoots are a paradise of pomegranates*
          with excellent fruit,
          henna blossoms with nard plants,

14   *nard and saffron, calamus and cinnamon,*
          with all trees of frankincense,
          myrrh and aloes with all the choicest of spices,

15   *a garden fountain, a well of living water*
          and streams flowing from Lebanon.

Bride to King

16   *Awake, O north wind.*
          And come, wind of the south.
          Blow upon my garden and let its spices flow forth.
          May my beloved come to his garden and eat
             its excellent fruit.

King to Bride

5:1   *I have come into my garden, my sister, my bride.*
I have gathered my myrrh with my balsam.
I have eaten my honeycomb with my honey.
I have drunk my wine with my milk.

The delicate shyness is conveyed by the indirect and poetic nature of his request, by her similar invitation and by his final declaration. What I mean is this: First, he compares her to a lovely garden and fountain (4:12-15). But the fountain is sealed and the garden is locked (4:12). This is a poetic way to praise her virginity and at the same time gently to request that she give herself to him. The door to her garden had been locked to all others so that one night she might give herself to her husband. Now that night had come.

After he elaborates on the garden and fountain imagery, she responds in the same imagery and invites him to come into her garden (4:16). Then after they have consummated their marriage, he declares that he has done so in the same imagery. "I have come into my garden" (5:1). So the imagery of the garden is present first in his request, then in her invitation and lastly in his declaration. An English teacher would call this an extended metaphor. But more important for us is that we feel the mood the poet is trying to communicate by this literary device.

Perhaps it would help to remember that when Shakespeare wished to communicate the same delicate mood in *Romeo and Juliet*, he employed this literary device also. The occasion was their first kiss. The imagery was a pilgrim on his pilgrimage. And the dialogue was as follows:

Romeo
If I profane with my unworthiest hand
This holy shrine, the gentle fine is this,
My lips, two blushing pilgrims, ready stand
To smooth that rough touch with a tender kiss.

Juliet
Good pilgrim, you do wrong your hand too much,
Which mannerly devotion shows in this;
For saints have hands that pilgrims' hands do touch,
And palm to palm is holy palmers kiss.
Romeo
Have not saints lips, and holy palmers too?
Juliet
Ay pilgrim, lips that they must use in prayer.
Romeo
O, then, dear saint, let lips do what hands do;
They pray, grant thou, lest faith turn to despair.
Juliet
Saints do not move, though grant for prayers' sake.
Romeo
Then move not, while my prayer's effect I take. (I, v, 95-109)
Harley Granville-Barker in *Prefaces to Shakespeare* remarks that "there is something sacramental in this ceremony, something shy and grave and sweet." The same could be said of the consummation in our song. It was sacramental, shy and grave and sweet. The mood was perfectly suited for the wedding night.

With a deeper awareness of this mood, the dialogue becomes all the more exquisite. After he compares her to a garden locked and a fountain sealed, he elaborates upon his description. First, he more fully describes the garden (4:13-14). Her garden is a paradise of delightful fruits, fragrant flowers, colorful blossoms, towering trees and aromatic spices. She is overwhelmingly beautiful, as re-freshing and uplifting as spring flowers and enchanting spices. She was the embodiment of the rich life of spring itself.

And as spring awakens winter's blacks and grays and whites to the multicolored life of a new world, so her loveliness awakened him from the black and white dullness of the ordinary to the colorful world of romance. Now he longed to fully possess his garden.

Yet he also expands upon the water imagery of the fountain, progressively increasing the level of his praise. The "fountain sealed" first mentioned would nourish one garden at most. Yet he next compares her to a spring of gardens which nourished many. Then he calls her a well of living water, and that might supply an entire city; yet streams flowing from Lebanon would prosper an entire countryside. So great is her refreshment to him that she can be likened to mountain streams which give life to an entire country-side.

So he offers the pinnacle of praise just before his bride offers her invitation to him. As the breezes of spring are the fragrant messengers of a garden sent to lure the outside world within, so she now requests those breezes to blow upon her garden and bring her lover to her. "Awake, O north wind. And come, wind of the south. Blow upon my garden and let its spices flow forth. May my beloved come to his garden and eat its excellent fruit." With poetic beauty and propriety she asks her lover to possess her. And when at last he does, it is "sacramental, shy and grave and sweet."

With exhilaration and hearty enjoyment, her new husband then declares, "I have come into my garden, my sister, my bride. I have gathered my myrrh with my balsam. I have eaten my honeycomb with my honey. I have drunk my wine with my milk." He describes their love as a beautiful garden he has enjoyed and as a great feast he has celebrated. Although the atmosphere was poetic and shy, the experience was certainly not placid or restrained.

It was poetic like a graceful ballerina is poetic—performing in carefully disciplined form, pausing and increasing speed as the music demands, yet exerting and enjoying the full release of her energies in the performance of the dance. It was an elegant, elegant wedding night.

He Is Now to Be among You at the Calling of Your Hearts
Nevertheless, the words of the lovers are not the last words of the night. A mysterious voice is the last to speak. "Eat, O loved ones; drink and be drunk, O lovers." Who is speaking to the lovers here? Some have suggested the wedding guests, but of course they are not likely to be around at this moment. And neither is any other person for that matter. Yet the voice must represent someone other than the lovers, for they are the ones addressed here.

A thorough search seems to leave us only two choices. Either it is the personified wind or it is God himself. The wind seems an unlikely candidate though the bride issued commands to it previously, it is true. But that can happen only because man is ruler over creation. For that very reason it would not be portrayed as superior to the couple, bidding them to enjoy their love.

Perhaps, however, these two choices at bottom are one. For even if the wind is speaking, it could only be saying the words its Creator prescribed. Nature hasn't the freedom to disobey. In the final analysis this must be the voice of the Creator, the greatest Poet, the most intimate wedding guest of all, the one, indeed, who prepared this lovely couple for the night of his design.

He lifts his voice and gives hearty approval to the entire night. He vigorously endorses and affirms the love of this couple. He takes pleasure in what has taken place. He is glad they have drunk deeply of the fountain of love. Two of his own have experienced love in all the beauty and fervor and purity that he intended for them. In fact, he urges them on to more. "Eat, O loved ones; drink and be drunk, O lovers." Eat together from the feast I have prepared for you. That is his attitude toward the giving of their love to each other.

And by the way, that's also his attitude toward couples today. Yet few couples seem to experience that kind of wedding night. Why is this so? Perhaps one reason is that their courtship does not prepare them for it. The couple in this song experienced a beautiful wedding night because they were prepared for it by a beautiful courtship. Perhaps we can look at their courtship and learn from them what romantic love should be like before marriage (1:1—3:11). After that we can move on to the account of their marriage and discover how such a love can blossom and grow continually (5:2—8:14).

JJ
The Birth of Romance

The event of falling in love. . . .
In one high bound it has overleaped
the massive wall of our selfhood;
it has made appetite itself altruistic,
tossed personal happiness
aside as a triviality and
planted the interests of another in
the centre of our being.
C. S. Lewis, The Four Loves

TWO

Often just a few choice snap-
shots can capture the flavor of a couple's relationship. One picture
may show them working together in overalls trying to paint the
playroom her father has just built. Still another may catch them
with a Christmas tree behind them as they sit upon a couch
together and gaze into a flickering fire in winter. Perhaps another
shows him in old jeans and a T-shirt, her in jeans and an old blouse,
both with tired eyes and a stack of school books in front of them.

A fourth shows the two holding hands and looking affection-
ately at one another at the senior prom. A fifth catches them in
graduation gowns and the funny flat hats. A sixth shows them
against the background of a large university building, looking
rather small and wide-eyed. A seventh reveals a girl looking more
like a woman and a boy looking more like a man while they're at
a fraternity dance.

An eighth picture shows him at a desk and her at a typewriter
as she helps him with his term paper. A ninth shows both of
them with cold red faces and bright eyes, each bundled up in ski

jackets and mittens as they stand huddled together in a lodge during Christmas vacation. Perhaps the tenth picture is an elegant one: he in a tuxedo standing in a church aisle and she in an exquisite white dress, lovely and happily standing beside her new husband. Just ten snapshots, but what a story they tell. It would be easy to put them in order and tell the story of their courtship.

In the same way that these ten snapshots capture the movement of their courtship, the poet of our song has arranged ten snapshots in order to tell the story of the courtship of the king and his bride. Let's look at each and see what we can learn from them.

The first snapshot is a picture of the king taken by the bride.

The Character of the King

1:2   *Oh, that he would kiss me with the kisses of his mouth,*
      for better than wine is your affection.

3   *For fragrance your perfumes are pleasing,*
      and perfume poured forth is your name.
      Therefore, the maidens love you.

4   *Draw me after you! Let us run together!*
      The king has brought me to his chambers.

Daughters of Jerusalem to King
      We will rejoice and be glad in you.
      We will extol your love (better) than wine.

Bride (in soliloquy)
      Rightly do they love you.

This picture was taken skillfully enough to capture the first reflections of both his role in their relationship and the inner character that lay behind that role. It seems at least here that he occupies a role of leadership, a role that she not only accepts but encourages. She asks that he may kiss her, not that she may initiate in kissing him. She asks that he may draw her after him so then they can run together. And it is he who began the relationship in bringing her to the palace chambers where they might see each other more often He arranged things so that they could be together. So he is the leader in their relationship, and although all the aspects of his leadership role may not be crystal clear in this picture, at least we see its beginnings.

We see the character behind the role when she says, "For fragrance your perfumes are pleasing, and perfume poured forth is your name. Therefore, the maidens love you." Evidently she liked his cologne, but she liked his character as well. In her culture a person's name often captured his character like our nicknames do sometimes. We may call a stern or stable person, Rock, or we may call a swift track man, Bullet. In her culture, however, character names were much more common than in ours. The name of the father of her nation meant "Father of a Multitude"; the name of one great general meant "Deliverer."

So when she said that his name was "perfume poured forth," she meant that his character was as fragrant and refreshing as cologne poured out of a bottle. This is the reason the girls around the palace loved him—not just because he was handsome though that he was, but because his inner person was so attractive.

People who knew him loved to talk about what a fine person he was, about how he loved and cared. We see his popularity when we hear the women of the court (called the Daughters of Jerusalem) say, "We will rejoice and be glad in you. We will extol your love (better) than wine." And because his character was so attractive, the girl who will someday be his bride can confidently say that the women of the court *rightly* appreciate him. After they praise him, she must agree, "Rightly do they love you."

What she says might seem to be a trite thing. But there is really an important lesson to be drawn from her appreciation of his character, and her recognition that it is right to love him. A girl today should be able to say the same things about the boy she may someday marry. Generally speaking, she should not be the only person in the world who sees what a good person her potential mate is. She should not be so infatuated that she imagines a scoundrel or knave to be her knight in shining armor. She should be able to say, "rightly do I love you." He should be the kind of person one ought to respect. For if he is not, she may find it much more difficult to respond to his leadership.

The Character of His Bride

The second snapshot is the picture of the girl who will one day be his bride.

Bride to Daughters of Jerusalem

1:5   *Dark am I but lovely, O daughters of Jerusalem,*
      like the tents of Kedar,
      like the curtains of Solomon.

6   *Do not stare at me for I am dark;*
      the sun has scorched me.
    My mother's sons were angry with me.
    They appointed me caretaker of the vineyards,
      but of my own vineyard—which belongs to me—
    I have not taken care.

(in soliloquy)

7   *Tell me, O you whom my soul loves,*
      where you pasture your flock,
      where you rest them at noon,
      lest I become as a veiled woman by the flocks
        of your companions.

Daughters of Jerusalem to Bride

8   *If you do not know, O most beautiful among women,*
      go forth on the trail of the flock
      and pasture your young goats by the tents
        of the shepherds.

As the first snapshot of the king revealed his character, so the second picture of his bride reveals much of her character. She is a bit self-conscious around the girls of the palace. Perhaps she feels that her darkened complexion marks her as a common laborer beside the fair-skinned girls of the palace. She is made more self-conscious as the women of the court stare at her.

She explains that her "mother's sons" (probably a term for her stepbrothers) were angry with her. As a result they forced her to work out in the fields where the sun beat down upon her. There she was unable to take care of herself like the girls of the palace. Of course she might feel uneasy around them!

Yet she has a natural attractiveness to her and a certain humility which often only suffering can bring. No doubt such genuineness and humility were refreshing changes for the king.

And she had a character he had to respect too. Remember she makes the request, "Tell me, O you whom my soul loves, where you pasture your flock, where you rest them at noon, lest I become as a veiled woman by the flocks of your companions." In their culture this term, "a veiled woman," referred to a loose girl, likely a prostitute. If she were going to see the king, she wanted it to be at the proper time and place—say, for example, when he was free in the middle of the day.

She didn't want to go wandering around looking for him, appearing to be an aggressive and available prostitute to everyone else. She didn't want to do anything that would even appear to compromise her feelings about what was right and wrong.

The character exhibited here as our model is perhaps the first lesson drawn for us from this portrait. Her humility coupled with her desire to do what was right is a simple but profitable ideal for any girl to follow.

Yet even in this picture of the bride we still catch another glimpse of the character of the king. Although he is a king, he is also like a shepherd. It may be he actually had flocks, but mainly he had a shepherd's strong and gentle character.

Frequently in love songs of their age, the lovers would play roles that reflected how they wanted to relate to one another. It was much like children (and adults) who playfully pretend to be hero and heroine, doctor and nurse, father and daughter, and all the rest. Perhaps she pictured him as a shepherd only to display his shepherdlike character, though he may have actually been a shepherd.

A shepherd worked long hours with little pay, yet he was often much admired for the sympathetic and understanding care he gave to his sheep. He had to deal with each one individually, inspecting each for bruises or more serious injuries. He had to be very gentle. Yet he needed to be very strong too. Often at the risk of his own life he would defend his flock against wild animals. The patient gentleness and courageous strength of a shepherd blended to form an admirable character. The king was like this. She appreciated it for she evidently liked him in that role.

Yet her appreciation of that reveals more about her. She appreciated the right things. And this provides another lesson to be drawn for us. Our values in courtship need to be right too.

The strange story has sometimes been told about the band of thieves who broke into a department store and stole nothing. They simply exchanged all the price tags. Some of the costliest items were priced very low, and some of the cheapest items were priced very high. An attractive, durable suit sold for $1.98; an exquisite oil painting was a dime; a well-made and dependable Swiss watch was 39 cents.

On the other hand, imitation jewelry was $600.00; cheap prints of the oil paintings were $700.00; bright plastic watches for children were $400.00. But strangest of all is that the next morning, and indeed for all the mornings after, the customers paid the new prices for all the items. What a ridiculous sight.

But it was no more ridiculous than the world in which we live. The price tags have all been exchanged on the qualities to look for in a potential husband or wife. We put a $1.98 tag on the durable qualities of character which like a good suit will wear well through the labor of life. A dime is what we would give for the inner beauty of a virtuous character which like a good painting can be enjoyed for a lifetime. We take the 39-cent price tag and put it on those qualities like dependability which like a good Swiss watch can always be counted upon to do the job that is required in spite of the adverse circumstance of a few bumps and a little bit of water.

We would rather set the $600.00 value on some cheap imitation phoniness because like its jewelry counterpart it is flashy and attracts attention. A $700.00 value goes for cheap prints of real character because we ourselves are so unskilled in judging art that we can't tell the difference. And a $400.00 price goes to the bright colors of prestige and position. But as the bright plastic band doesn't enable the children's watch to work, so this bright fringe benefit doesn't enable a relationship to work. Our values need to be properly placed as were those of the girl who married the shepherdlike king.

His Love Makes Me Beautiful
The last snapshot pictured the character of the future bride. There we saw that her long hours of work in the vineyards had prevented her properly caring for herself. And because she had little money for clothes and jewelry, she could not dress as well as other girls in the palace. With inferiority plaguing her, she was actually a bit insecure.

In this third snapshot, however, we see the first steps taken in overcoming that insecurity and making her feel loved and at home in the royal court. In this picture one sees a lovely girl standing silently as the king and some other girls in the palace are speaking to her.

King to Bride

1:9   *To a mare among the chariots of Pharaoh*
          I liken you my darling.

10   *Lovely are your cheeks with ornaments*
         and your neck with strings of beads.

Daughters of Jerusalem to Bride

11   *Chains of gold will we make for you*
         with points of silver.

When his future bride looked at herself, she was conscious only of her neglected appearance. But when the king looked at her, it was a look of love since he saw the most wonderful girl in the world. And he didn't keep that feeling to himself. He says, "To a mare among the chariots of Pharaoh I liken you my darling."

The chariots of Pharaoh were pulled by several pairs of horses, but the prize mare led the chariot all alone. That mare was uniquely noble and beautiful among the rest. So was this girl in the heart of the king. If she could just see herself through the eyes of the king, her own view of herself could not stay the same. Perhaps later snapshots of her will show the effects his praise had upon her.

She is also aware of her inadequate dress for the palace for she has never owned the clothes necessary for that life. Realizing this need of hers, the king tells her that she looks very lovely in the new jewelry she will soon have as her own. At this point the ladies of the court offer to make that jewelry for her.

It is very interesting to notice how helpful these ladies have become since they have seen how the king cared for her. In the last picture when she asks where the king pastured his flock at noon, they may have been almost sarcastic in their answer, "If you do not know, O most beautiful among women, go forth on the trail of the flock and pasture your young goats by the tents of the shepherds" (1:8). Yet such wandering was the very thing she did not want to do. Now, however, their respect for her has increased for they see how important she is to the king.

Isn't there a good lesson to draw from the king's action in this picture? He is sensitive to the needs of the girl he loves. So he verbally assures her of the special place she has in his heart, and he sees to it that she is provided all that is necessary to make her feel at home in her new surroundings. And so respected was he in the court that his love for her gave her a position of respect as well. It is not surprising that he came to have a special place in her heart too. The next snapshot shows how special it was.

Cherish Is the Word I Use to Describe

When some girls think of the boys they date, they wince their eyes and groan, "How could I be stuck with such a clod? He's inconsiderate, crude and sarcastic, and it's really almost nice when he leaves town for a while." Such is the attitude of some girls who make unfortunate decisions about one guy and are then too lazy or insecure to try to correct the situation. But the lovely girl of our song knew what true love was all about.

She was happy just to think about him. It was refreshing to remember the fine person he was as well as the things he had done for her. Our fourth snapshot has captured her in one of these moments. The king is sitting at the royal dining table to eat. Perhaps it is filled with dignitaries and officials buzzing over national affairs, and perhaps the women of the court are chatting over the latest events on the social calendar. All the talk and the people fade into the background for her, however, as she looks past them and sees only the one she loves. And when she contemplates him, she cannot help but smile softly from her thoughts.

1:12 *While the king was at his table,*
my nard gave its fragrance.

13   *A pouch of myrrh is my beloved to me*
      which lies all night between my breasts.
14   *My beloved is to me a cluster of henna blossoms*
      in the vineyards of En-Gedi.

Nard is one of many kinds of myrrh. It is as if she said something like, "While the king was at his table, my Chanel gave its fragrance; a sachet of perfume is my beloved to me which lies all night between my breasts." It was common in her culture for a woman to wear a little pouch of perfume around her neck which would constantly produce a fragrant aroma for her. Evidently, she wore one of these containers of perfume around her neck too.

While the king was dining, her perfume still gave its fragrance. But the perfume in this case represents her lover for she says he is the pouch of myrrh, the sachet of perfume. So while she contemplates him at the table, her thoughts of him are as fragrant and refreshing as the perfume that rises before her. Notice that he is not forgotten either when night brings separation. The perfume lies all night between her breasts. She also carries those fragrant thoughts of him through the night in peaceful sleep.

Yet her appreciation of him seems to be even deeper in her next words: "My beloved is to me a cluster of henna blossoms in the vineyards of En-Gedi." En-Gedi was an oasis in a desert wilderness. All around it were hot, dry sands extending monotonously for miles, and nowhere in all that desert could anything grow. Then suddenly one comes upon En-Gedi. It is green and bright and fresh, a welcome sight to any traveler. The king was like En-Gedi to this girl, an oasis of life in a desert of monotony, and like a weary traveler she found refreshment with him.

But even more precious than an oasis in the desert, he was like the loveliest flowers in that oasis, the delicate henna blossoms. He was indeed very special to her. But it was right that he should be because she was in love with him. She would probably marry him, and to feel less strongly about him would cast doubt on the advisability of marriage.

You Make Me Feel Brand New

The fifth snapshot of their courtship is the first picture which depicts the two of them conversing together. A long-range lens was necessary for this one because they were on one of their frequent walks in the country. When they sat down to rest under the trees, the photographer took this one. They are looking into each other's eyes as they speak to one another.

King to Bride

1:15   *Behold, you are beautiful my darling; behold you*
       are beautiful;
       Your eyes are doves.

Bride to King

16   *Behold, you are handsome my beloved; indeed you are pleasant.*
       And our couch is verdant.

17   *The beams of our houses are cedars;*
       our rafters, cypresses.

2:1   *I am a rose of Sharon,*
       a lily of the valley.

King to Bride

2   *As a lily among thorns,*
       thus is my darling among the young women.

Bride (to King)

3   *As an apple tree among the trees of the forest,*
       so is my beloved among the young men.
    In his shade I took great delight and sat down,
       and his fruit was sweet to my taste.

We can see from this picture that the couple has become much closer to one another. They are more relaxed and freer to express their appreciation than during her first days at the palace. In fact, this is the first time in the snapshots that we have seen anything like an extended conversation between them.

It is difficult for two people to hold back their true feelings for each other—almost painful to love and not be able to express it. Without a doubt he is happy to express more fully his love for her. He is glad he can tell her she is beautiful and her eyes are like doves. She responds with a similar compliment, telling him that he is handsome but adding that he is pleasant too. Evidently they are at home among nature because she also says that their couch is the grass, the beams of their house are cedars, and the rafters, cypresses. The grass and the cedars and the cypresses form the home of their courtship. In this woodland setting she sees herself as a rose of Sharon, a lily of the valley. (Sharon was a fertile, coastal plain in northern Palestine.)

Isn't it interesting how her view of herself has changed since her first days at the palace? Then she was self-conscious of her appearance: "Do not stare at me for I am dark; the sun has scorched me. My mother's sons were angry with me. They appointed me caretaker of the vineyards, but of my own vineyard—which belongs to me—I have not taken care." Now, however, she sees herself as a rose of Sharon, a lily of the valley. What has caused this transformation? It must be that she has at last begun to see herself through his eyes. Her self-image has risen because she sees herself as he sees her, so she claims to be a rose of Sharon, a lily of the valley.

But he will not allow her to stop there in her evaluation of herself. She is not just a lily of the valley. "As a lily among thorns," he adds, "thus is my darling among the young women." She is unique among all the rest, as distinct from them as a lily among thorns.

She then returns a similar compliment to him. "As an apple tree among the trees of the forest, so is my beloved among the young men." He is also uniquely special to her. But she adds, as if to excel his praise of her, "In his shade I took great delight and sat down, and his fruit was sweet to my taste." Whereas before she came to him she worked long hours in the sun (1:6), now she rests under the protective shade that he brings. And although formerly she was so exhausted by her work she could not properly care for herself, now she finds time for refreshment with him. Every girl who falls in love should find such rest in the one she loves. And she should find such rest in no one else.

III
The Flower
of
Courtship

This bud of love
by summer's ripening breath
may prove
a beauteous flower
when next we meet.
William Shakespeare,
Romeo and Juliet

THREE

The next few snapshots of their courtship reveal a steady movement toward their marriage. Twice we shall see a cycle of longing, patience and reward bring their relationship to loftier plateaus. The first cycle begins with a picture of them in the palace banquet hall. She looks radiantly happy and very much in love.

I Love How You Love Me
Bride (in soliloquy)

2:4 *He has brought me to the banquet hall,*
and his banner over me is love.

(to King)

5 *Sustain me with raisin cakes and refresh me with apples*
for I am faint with love.

(in soliloquy)

6 *Oh that his left hand were under my head and his right hand*
embraced me.

to Daughters of Jerusalem

7   *I adjure you, O daughters of Jerusalem,*
        by the gazelles or the hinds of the field
        not to arouse, not to awaken love until it pleases.

When she says, "His banner over me is love," do you think that she
means her lover carried a football fan's banner with "love" written
upon it held high above her head? Probably not. The banner she
speaks of refers to that high, wide banner that was used in battle.
When the troops needed to regroup, this banner was raised so that
all could see where to go. This kind of banner was also used in great
marches where thousands of people were divided up and guided
by the position of the banner. It served as a gigantic traveling
billboard.

Are you beginning to understand what this girl is saying? She is
proclaiming that the love which the king has for her is evident to
everyone. He does not say one thing to her in private and contradict
that in public. He is not warm and considerate when they are alone
but cold and sarcastic when they are with others. He is not ashamed
of his love for her, so he is glad for all to see it. No wonder she grew
more and more secure in his love.

She even becomes lovesick, weak from her growing devotion to
this man. So she says, "Sustain me with raisin cakes and refresh me
with apples for I am faint with love." Because she loves him so
much, she longs to express it to him physically and to be embraced
by him. "Oh that his left hand were under my head and his right
hand embraced me." It is easy to see that the only way for his left
hand to be under her head and his right hand to embrace her would
be if they were lying down. Actually this wish is very similar to
requests in other songs of this age in which a girl asks to make love
to her husband. This is no doubt what she means.

From her wish, an excellent principle can be drawn for courtship. A strong desire to express love physically should be present,

but not until marriage should it be fulfilled. This restraint is healthy and beneficial to the couple. Psychologists tell us that repression is harmful because repression is the subconscious attempt to pretend that you don't have certain feelings. It would be wrong for this girl to pretend that she does not have a strong desire to make love to the man who would soon be her husband.

But nothing is wrong with suppression—the conscious restraint of natural impulses. For example, you may have an impulse to hit someone in the nose, but it is good to suppress that impulse and restrain yourself. As they come closer to marriage, restraint becomes more necessary.

Hence the next words of this bride-to-be are words of advice to be patient. "I adjure you... by the gazelles or the hinds of the field not to arouse, not to awaken love until it pleases." One should not force the development of love. One should not try to awaken love until love pleases. Trying to force love to develop would be like trying to force a flower to blossom—it could only tear the petals. But when a flower blossoms naturally, it is very beautiful. Thus it is with love. So this was very timely advice for the girl herself. She was already to the point where she wanted to marry this man and give herself to him. Yet, she realized that she could not force the relationship to develop faster than its natural course would take. Love would awaken and progress when it pleased. She could not force it to awaken. So after experiencing the most intense longing of her courtship she gives sound advice to be patient.

Color My World

It probably seemed like forever until their relationship grew to the point where she wished it would be. Love makes clocks worthless and calendars deceiving. A few days between phone calls sometimes seems like months. And we cannot even remember when it was we last had time alone with the one we love. Yet it may have been only a week. Then before we know it, we find ourselves together and much closer to that one than ever before.

No doubt this young girl shares with all of us the experience of trying to be patient. Yet one bright spring day she found herself together with him in their most delightful time thus far, a fine reward for her patience. Luckily for us, someone took a snapshot of them on this day. And in color! All the bright reds and yellows and pastels of spring show up well; everything seems overflowing with life, and nothing seems more full of life than the couple in the center of the picture.

Bride (in soliloquy)

2:8   *The sound of my beloved,*
      Behold, he is coming,
        leaping over the mountains, bounding over the hills.

9   *My beloved is like a gazelle or a young stag.*
      Look, he is standing behind our wall,
        gazing through the windows,
        peering through the lattice.

10   *My beloved responded and said to me,*
      "Arise my darling, my fair one, and come.

11   *For behold, the winter has passed.*
      The rain is over and gone.

12   *The blossoms have appeared in the land.*
      The time of singing has come,
        and the cooing of the turtle dove is heard in our land.

13   *The fig tree forms its figs,*
      and the vines in blossom give forth fragrance.
    Arise, my darling, my beautiful one, and come along.

14   *O my dove, in the clefts of the rocks,*
      in the hidden places of the steep pathway,
    Let me see your form; let me hear your voice.
    For your voice is sweet, and your form is lovely."

Notice her excitement at hearing her beloved. "Behold, he is coming." And he is evidently very excited too. She says he is "like a gazelle or a young stag" that is "leaping over the mountains, bounding over the hills." I suppose if he lived today he would come bounding down the stairs, speed through the front door with a slam and be off in his car in a hurry to see his girlfriend.

Yet both the modern boy and the king act the same way when they arrive. "Look, he is standing behind our wall, gazing through the windows, peering through the lattice." He probably knocked first, then when she didn't respond immediately, he put his hands to his eyes and tried to look through the window to see if she were there. He couldn't wait to see her.

Then he grabs her hand and practically pulls her outside to the beautiful spring day, urging her to come along with him to enjoy it. "Arise my darling, my fair one, and come. For behold, the winter has passed. The rain is over and gone. The blossoms have appeared in the land. The time of singing has come, and the cooing of the turtledove is heard in our land. The fig tree forms its figs, and the vines in blossom give forth fragrance. Arise, my darling, my beautiful one, and come along."

What a perfect background for their relationship—the fragrance of spring, the beauty of its flowers, the sound of birds singing. As the poet Coleridge wrote, when love comes "the trees whisper, the roses exhale their perfumes, the nightingales sing, nay the very skies smile in unison with the feeling of true and pure love."

Have you ever wondered why spring has always been the season for lovers, the background of romantic literature in every century? It must be because the season of spring reflects the experience of the young lovers. Everything is fresh; new life flows through the world; happiness and colors triumph over winter's boring grays. Whenever any couple falls in love, it is spring for them because their lives are fresh; everything in life has a new perspective; what was black and white is now in color; what was dark is light.

I remember in high school it would often happen that one who was formerly a rather ordinary girl would suddenly become noticeably attractive almost overnight. We of the "girl-watchers' brigade" would ask ourselves why we had never noticed her before. The answer was simple. We hadn't seen this brand new version. She had fallen in love and it had transformed her appearance. She was happier, better dressed and a much more lovely person. Too late for any of us, but the lesson remained—new love brings new life. Spring lovers, like spring trees, though plain and barren in winter, become full and lovely in spring.

One good indication of real love is the desire to communicate, a wish to discover all about this person whom you love so much. No detail seems too trivial to be related. No mood or feeling of one is unimportant to the other. And you care about the details and the feelings because you care so much about the person. That which would be insignificant or boring to even a good friend is eagerly received with genuine interest by the one who loves you. Love will produce this concern. But this takes time, of course—lingering time where floating thoughts can unhurriedly and unthreateningly be expressed and unmeasured time where quiet reflection may confidently precede the replies of conversation. Love seeks a time and place for this, as a song from a modern musical agrees, "There's a place for us, a time and place for us. Time together with time to spare, time to learn, time to care, somewhere."

The couple in our song of songs found a time and place for this. After describing the lovely spring day, the king goes on to say to her, "O my dove, in the clefts of the rocks, in the hidden places of the steep pathway, let me see your form; let me hear your voice. For your voice is sweet, and your form is lovely."

The doves would often hide in the rocks on the mountains and one could not see or hear them. The girl whom he loved was somewhat like this. She was hidden not only because she may still have been inside the house but because her voice had spoken too infrequently to him. He longed to know her better, to see her and to hear the words she would speak.

However, a fact is implicit in his request that all young lovers intuitively know. The mere voice of the one loved is enchantingly special just in itself. One could read from the telephone book and the other would raptly listen simply for the sound of the voice.

I remember one time I was studying through this song with Jackie Deere, a close friend, and right before we came to this verse, he leaned back in his chair and asked what I thought about the voice of the girl I was dating at the time. Not having read on, I didn't know the reason he had asked. But I congratulated both of us on being so sensitive to the songlike quality of her voice. Then I proudly went on and on about the virtues of such a voice.

When I paused to catch my breath, he matter of factly said, "Well, I haven't noticed anything special about it really, but the next verse indicates that the voice of the one you love is very special." Thanks a lot. I got the point, however, and I haven't quite been able to forget the way I learned it.

It is true, though, that the little things are greatly appreciated by those in love—details of experiences, shades of feelings and even the sound of the voice. This snapshot of our couple reveals they appreciated and enjoyed such things. It also concludes the first cycle of longing, patience and reward.

A Very Precious Love

Before the second cycle begins there is an interlude which captures the effects of their deeper experiences of love in the previous picture of spring. First the king speaks to his loved one.

2:15   *"Let us catch the foxes—the little foxes who ruin vineyards,*
for our vineyards are in blossom."

Bride (in soliloquy)

16   *My beloved is mine and I am his—he who pastures his flock*
       among the lilies.

17   *Until the day breathes and the shadows flee,*
       turn, my beloved, and be like a gazelle or a
       young stag on the mountains of separation.

As their relationship becomes more precious to them, they place
a much higher value upon it. They want more than anything else
to protect and preserve it. The king wisely realizes that all kinds
of things could threaten or destroy it. Hence he resolves with her,
"Let us catch the foxes—the little foxes who ruin vineyards, for our
vineyards are in blossom." Elsewhere in the song, "vineyards"
have referred to a person (1:6; 8:12). It seems that also in this request
"our vineyards" refers to the lovers themselves. "While their vineyards are in blossom" refers to this time while they are in the love
of courtship. At this time they need to catch the foxes that ruin vineyards. They need to catch anything that might destroy their relationship of love.

How appropriate is that determination now! Usually flowers
blossom only at certain times of the year. During that season, especially, one needs to guard against the foxes. And now it is that
special time in the lives of these young lovers when they are in
blossom from love. Of course, even before they met one another,
they should have been concerned that "foxes" would not harm
them, but now in the time of blossom it is especially important to
guard against anything that would spoil their relationship.

The foxes represent as many obstacles or temptations as have
plagued lovers throughout the centuries. Perhaps it is the fox of
uncontrolled desire which drives a wedge of guilt between a
couple. Perhaps it is the fox of mistrust and jealousy which breaks
the bond of love. Or it may be the fox of selfishness and pride which
refuses to let one acknowledge his fault to another. Or it may be an

unforgiving spirit which will not accept the apology of the other. These foxes have been ruining vineyards for years and the end of their work is not in sight.

Notice the king does not say "let me" catch the foxes, but rather "let us." Both must resolve to protect and preserve their love. And their deeper experience of love captured in the last picture surely motivated them to do just that.

But it also gave them a wonderful and fulfilling experience of mutual belongingness. His bride-to-be can affirm, "My beloved is mine and I am his—he who pastures his flock among the lilies." True love should bring this experience—not "I am his and he is everyone's," nor "He is mine, and Teddy is mine, and Joel is mine, and Ken is mine, and so forth." The belongingness is mutual. The commitment is mutual. The couple can say, "We belong to each other."

Some people have the mistaken idea that they can be happy only with a partner who is the best-looking, most intelligent, most sensitive person in the world. Or they must have the closest to that they could get considering what this "perfect" partner was receiving in return.

But this verse reveals that love will be found not in the one who rates the highest on your set of standards, but in the one you feel belongs to you. You don't look at the other person as a status symbol who will raise your level of prestige; having accepted yourself, you look at that one as your counterpart, the one who completes you, the one with whom you can joyfully affirm your belongingness.

Isn't it interesting that when she affirms her belongingness to him she explicitly adds, "He who pastures his flock among the lilies." She is drawing attention to his shepherd role wherein he would pasture his flock. And by this she emphasizes his shepherd-like qualities of strength and gentleness. He was strong and masculine; she was tender and feminine; but both were gentle. They belonged to one another.

But they longed to belong to one another physically as well. So after she affirms their belongingness with "My beloved is mine and I am his," she expresses her desire to be his completely. Yet as a lady she is neither crude nor blunt but poetic in her request. "Until the day breathes and the shadows flee, turn, my beloved, and be like a gazelle or a young stag on the mountains of separation." The mountains of separation are, as we have seen before, likely to be a subtle reference to her breasts, and the day would breathe at dawn when the shadows of darkness would flee.

She is asking him in a beautiful way to one day consummate their marriage in a wedding night lasting until dawn. We have seen that when that night comes, he does indeed verbally answer this request and fulfill it (4:6). Thus the eighth picture from their courtship, this interlude in the longing, patience, reward cycle, has revealed that their deeper romance has fostered not only a desire to protect it, but also a confidence of belongingness which longs for fulfillment in marriage.

It's By Far the Hardest Thing I've Ever Done

Anytime anything really important is about to happen in a person's life, he will face all sorts of hopes and fears. Before the championship game, an athlete may lie in bed all night just thinking about what will happen. He may be unusually fearful of even remote problems. What if somehow or another he fails to get to the game on time because of car failure? What if he loses his jersey or gets sick or fails to perform like he always has? One reason all these fears emerge may be because the athlete wants to win so badly that his fear of losing increases proportionately. When a person dreams about such failures, a psychologist calls them fear-fulfillment dreams. Similarly, when you love a person very much, you may dream the person is taken from you. It is a fear-fulfillment dream.

Just before the great event of marriage, the bride-to-be of our song has an experience of this sort. The narration of it indicates it may be a dream. But whether dream or not, it illustrates the intensity of her love for her future husband. So deep is her love that the fear of losing him produces great anxiety.

3:1   *Upon my bed in the night I sought him whom my soul*
           loves.

           I sought him but did not find him.

2   *I will arise now and go about in the city,*
           in the streets and in the squares.

           I will seek him whom my soul loves.

           I sought him but did not find him.

3   *The watchmen who go about in the city found me.*

           (I said), "Have you seen him whom my soul loves?"

4   *Scarcely had I passed from them when I found him*
           whom my soul loves.

           I held on to him and would not let him go
           until I brought him to the house of my mother,
           to the room of the one who conceived me.

to the Daughters of Jerusalem

5   *I adjure you, O daughters of Jerusalem,*
           by the gazelles or the hinds of the field
           not to arouse, not to awaken love until it pleases.

Four times in the first four verses she refers to her future husband as "him whom my soul loves." From her innermost self she reached out for him but he was not there. No doubt she might have been told that she could wait at least until the next day. She previously had weeks to wait. Why was it so urgent now?

The persons who may have scorned her urgency had forgotten what it was like to be so much in love and on the verge of marriage. They had forgotten that time together was timeless, that time apart was an eternity. They had forgotten that to be so soon separated from one so soon found—and in finding having found oneself as well—was like the rending apart of a single person, the tearing away of one without whom you now felt more lonely and empty and helpless than ever possible before you met. They had simply forgotten this: Love not only brings a greater experience of joy but a deeper capacity for pain as well. So as the joy of the king's presence became greater, so the sorrow from his absence became deeper.

That is why she anxiously and urgently sought "him whom her soul loved" without waiting until the next day. Instead of sleeping she tossed and turned and thought only of seeing him. "Upon my bed in the night I sought him whom my soul loves. I sought him but did not find him." She had to get up and find him, so she says to herself, "I will arise now and go about in the city, in the streets and in the squares. I will seek him whom my soul loves."

While she looks for him she comes across the men who guard the city at night. When these watchmen find her, they help her find the king. Hence she says, "The watchmen who go about in the city found me. (I said), 'Have you seen him whom my soul loves?' Scarcely had I passed from them when I found him whom my soul loves."

When a person is insecure or anxious about someone or something, it is natural to want to go to a place which he associates with security and stability. Therefore, home is a great place to go after a disorienting and hectic trip or a lonely and depressing experience away at college. It is natural in times of anxiety to want to go to a place where one always felt secure, where everything was okay.

Understandably, then, after fearing the loss of her fiancé, and finding him, this young girl takes him to her own home. "I held on to him and would not let him go until I brought him to the house of my mother, to the room of the one who conceived me." She was like a very young girl who waking up after a bad dream and being assured that all is well, nevertheless, still crawls under the covers of her mother to sleep until the lingering fears are past. One's heart beats fast even after imminent danger is over. Hence, only the time holding on to him at her own home would bring her fearful heart to rest.

But after she comes to rest and realizes that all is well, she very wisely gives counsel to others and herself to be patient. She repeats the very same advice she previously gave when her own longing and the courtship had itself reached new peaks. "I adjure you, O daughters of Jerusalem, by the gazelles or the hinds of the field not to arouse, not to awaken love until it pleases." In other words, let the flower blossom in its proper season.

In the first cycle of their courtship, the pattern emerged of their longing, patience and reward. Their previous reward was the deepest experience of love that they had experienced to that point. But now the second cycle is concluded with an even greater reward —the wedding day itself. The very next snapshot of their courtship is a very professional picture of their wedding procession.

The Wedding Song

In nearly every culture in the world, the great events of life are marked by ceremony and tradition. Birth, marriage, death—traditions surround them all. Sometimes in our culture a person may go to church only three times in his life—when he is baptized, when he is married and when he is buried. This is man's recognition that these events are truly important. Marriage marks the entrance into a whole new way of life; in fact, it is a new life according to the Scripture for one new life is created in marriage when the two become one.

Of course, recently in our culture it has become popular to minimize the newness of this life by casually living together with prospective mates before marriage. The marriage, then, is anticlimactic because it no longer stands for the embarking upon a whole new life together. But where a couple recognizes that marriage is important and lasting and where they long to give themselves only to each other forever, then the wedding has the great significance it should have.

Because marriage was so important to the couple in our song and because they had patiently waited to give themselves to each other on this day, their wedding had all the significance and importance it was intended to represent. They were not pretending that this day would begin a new life for them; they knew it actually would begin a new life for them. And like most modern couples they were careful to preserve pictures of this day in their lives. The picture presented to us in the song is of the wedding procession:

3:6   *What is this coming from the wilderness*
        like columns of smoke,
        from the burning of myrrh and frankincense
        made from all the scented powders of the merchant?

7   *Behold! It is the couch of Solomon.*
        Sixty mighty men around it from the mighty men of Israel.

8   *All of them wielders of the sword, trained for battle;*
        Each, his sword at his side
        (for protection) from the terrors of the night.

9   *A palanquin King Solomon made for himself*
        from the timber of Lebanon.

10   *He made its posts of silver, its back of gold,*
        its seat of purple cloth, its interior inlaid
        with expressions of love from the daughters of Jerusalem.

11   *Go forth, O daughters of Zion, and look upon King Solomon*
        with the crown with which his mother has crowned him
        on the day of his wedding
        and on the day of the gladness of his heart.

Actually it is not until the last verse that the reader is sure that this is the wedding procession. There the reader is asked to look upon the king "with the crown with which his mother has crowned him on the day of his wedding." Up to that point the grandeur of the groom had been emphasized. Most of us are used to all the eyes being on the bride in the procession, but here all the focus is on the groom.

Off in the distance one sees first a large and indistinct cloud of dust marching closer and closer. But it is a royal dust, rising clouds of myrrh and frankincense. As the procession comes closer and closer, the poet exclaims, "Behold! It is the couch of Solomon." The king was being carried on something like a traveling chair. And did he ever have a large wedding!

Twelve groomsmen is the most I have ever seen. Yet it was written of this traveling couch "sixty mighty men around it from the mighty men of Israel. All of them wielders of the sword, trained for battle; each, his sword at his side (for protection) from the terrors of the night."

This is a full-dress military wedding and all the king's best soldiers are in their finest uniforms. This picture really emphasizes the strength and importance of the king, his ability to protect and provide for his bride.

Being represented in this way, the king serves as a model for other grooms to follow. Not that they need sixty soldiers behind them when they marry, but they should have the same capacity to protect and provide for their bride. And it should be their heartfelt desire to do so. These soldiers weren't there to keep the king from backing out. Yet sometimes in present-day weddings, the grooms-men may have to keep a steady hand on the groom to make sure he doesn't head out the back door. And occasionally even sixty soldiers could not contain such a frantic groom.

But the king was not like this. He was eagerly anticipating his marriage. He had made special preparations for it like people do today. Notice that "a palanquin King Solomon made for himself

from the timber of Lebanon." The best timber was from up north in
Lebanon. Only the best was good enough for the king on this day.
"He made its posts of silver, its back of gold, its seat of purple
cloth."

It had to be made of the finest materials, and the king could not
reach higher for quality than to prepare this traveling couch from
the gold and silver from his treasury and the purple cloth repre-
sentative of royalty. He wanted to show forth the best he had. Yet
this attitude is not new to him for all through his courtship he has
set forth the noblest qualities of his character as well. And in doing
so he has really acted no differently than many lovers of any century.

Love and marriage frequently bring out the noblest qualities in a
person. A carefree and somewhat careless young man may become
very responsible and diligent. A childish boy may become steady
and manly. Why? Because love is the mother of virtue and the father
of maturity.

Now here is an important test of true love. The one you love
should bring forth your best qualities and make you a better person. It was very perceptive of one fellow I know to say of his fiancée,
"I love her not only because she is so wonderful but because of the
way I am when I am with her. She's such an encouragement to me to
be the right kind of person." She brought out a sense of direction
and responsibility and also a tenderness that he had seldom expressed before. No wonder all the world loves a lover—he is a
lovelier person.

And everyone likes to participate in the joyous event of his wedding. It is their way of sharing in his joy. Notice that the palanquin
that the king had made had "its interior inlaid with expressions
of love from the daughters of Jerusalem." They gladly worked to
make the palanquin very beautiful for the king. Their attitude was
not much different from many mothers and fathers and friends to-

day who gladly do everything they can to make the wedding a beautiful and memorable affair. Then with special pride all who helped can look upon the lovely wedding they helped prepare. Hence the poet concludes by saying, "Go forth, O daughters of Zion, and look upon King Solomon with the crown with which his mother has crowned him on the day of his wedding and on the day of his gladness of his heart."

It was not only the day of gladness for the king but also for those who shared in his happiness. And many there were that did. Their love had become a fountain from which all could taste the sweetness of their joy. No doubt it is the wish of the Creator of life that every romance prove to be such a fountain from which all can drink.

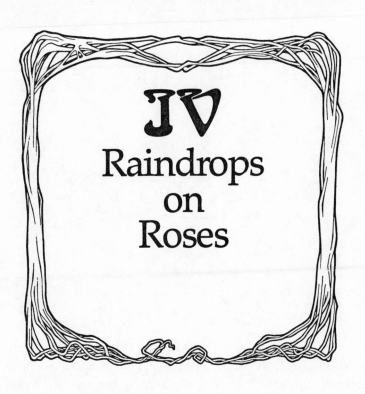

IV
Raindrops
on
Roses

Softly fell the raindrops
from the roses,
Gently fell the teardrops
from her cheeks.

FOUR

After the wedding procession which concluded their courtship came the wedding night which began their marriage. It was described in the first chapter, and it was truly beautiful. One might now expect the romance to conclude with "and they lived happily ever after." Perhaps a modern love story would end that way. But although this romance is an ideal, it is not a fantasy. It is realistic, and it presents the realistic problems of marriage. But it is also a model romance for others to follow, so thankfully it not only presents the problems of marriage but also the principles for solving them.

The first problem is presented immediately following the account of the wedding night. This does not mean, of course, that it occurred on the following day. We have already seen that the events in this song are arranged like snapshots in an album. They capture only the significant events of the relationship. And the next significant event in their life together after the wedding night was their first problem. Perhaps they remembered it because they did not expect it, and surprises are hard to forget. No doubt their honeymoon had lasted long; they likely thought it would last forever. But then—for who knows what reason—came the night when his love and devotion were met by her apathy and indifference.

Rainy Days and Mondays

Often the opposite of love appears not to be hate but indifference. If someone hates you, at least he regards you as a significant person. But if he is indifferent towards you, then he regards you as a zero. And indifference can hurt worse too.

What could be worse than to have your sincere declaration of love met by a yawn and a "You don't really mean that." The pain would cut deep and not be soon healed. And it would likely hurt all the more if the one lover were accustomed to a response of love. The husband in our song had indeed grown accustomed to a response of love from his new wife. Yet this night he was met with indifference. And such indifference signaled a break in the progress of their relationship.

Bride to Daughters of Jerusalem

5:2 *I was asleep but my heart was awake.*
The sound of my beloved knocking,
"Open to me my sister, my darling, my dove, my perfect one,
for my hair is filled with dew; my hair, with damp
of the night."

3 *I had put off my tunic; must I put it on again?*
I had washed my feet; must I soil them again?

4 *My beloved withdrew his hand from the door,*
and my feelings were aroused for him.

5 *I arose to open to my beloved*
and my hand dripped with myrrh
and my fingers with flowing myrrh upon the handles
of the bolt.

6 *I opened to my beloved, but my beloved had turned and gone.*

My soul had gone out to him when he spoke.
I sought him but did not find him;
I called out to him, but he did not answer me.
7   *The watchmen who go about in the city found me.*
They struck me; they bruised me.
They took my shawl from upon me—those guardians of the
walls.
8   *I adjure you, O daughters of Jerusalem,*
if you find my beloved—as to what you will tell him—
(tell him) that I am faint with love.

To make sure the reader understood, the poet of our song underscored the apathy of the wife in several ways. Whereas she has been comfortably in bed, her husband has been outside, perhaps working, for his hair has been "filled with dew." And the husband's fervent address to his wife is a startling contrast to her listless response. He says, "Open to me, my sister, my darling, my dove, my perfect one." Nowhere else in the song does he address her with so many affectionate terms.

It is the poet's way of telling us that the king is as full of love for his wife as he could be. "Sister" was an affectionate term designating one's wife; "darling" had been his name for her during courtship; but "dove" and "perfect one" were new terms of affection which gave full expression of his appreciation for her. Yet his words served only to provide an eloquent contrast to the apathetic response of his wife. "I had put off my tunic; must I put it on again? I had washed my feet; must I soil them again?"

Today the situation might have been that her husband had just come in from a long trip and she would say, "I've already gotten ready for bed; do I have to get up again? My hair is already in rollers; do you want me to unroll it now?" What a contrast this attitude is with her attitude just before the wedding day (3:1-4).

Then she couldn't sleep at night because she wanted to see him so badly. Then even the watchmen of the city helped her locate her beloved fiancé. Then she had to get up in the middle of the night and find him and not let go of him until her fearful heart was quieted. But now . . . she had forgotten that the whole purpose of her nightly beauty preparation was for him and that apart from him there was no reason to prepare.

In the Egyptian love songs of that era lovers frequently appear immature and sometimes even immoral in comparison with the lovers in the Song of Songs. Yet ironically one lover from the Egyptian love songs could have been an example to the wife of this song. One girl much in love says, "My heart remembers well your love, one-half of my hair was combed and I came rushing to see you and I forgot about my hair." This should have been the attitude of the king's new wife.

Yet in the midst of busily making herself a good wife, she forgot why and for whom she was doing it. Actually she was no different from many a modern housewife who becomes so involved in taking care of her husband's children and house that she forgets about her husband. Likewise, somewhere in the midst of her activity, the king's wife fell into an attitude of indifference. How would he respond?

Contrary to all expectations he does not become angry. His wife reports his response as follows, "My beloved withdrew his hand from the door, and my feelings were aroused for him. I arose to open to my beloved and my hand dripped with myrrh and my fingers with flowing myrrh upon the handles of the bolt. I opened to my beloved, but my beloved had turned and gone."

He simply left her a "love note" and then went away. In their culture a lover would leave this fragrant myrrh at the door as a sign that he had been there. Even the king could do this for his wife because she likely had her own special room in the palace. No anger. Just an affectionate reminder that he had come to see her.

That was his response before he left. He realized that his anger could not force love. He heeded the wise advice "not to arouse, not to awaken love until it pleases."

Actually his anger would only have confirmed her ungrateful attitude toward him. He wasn't anything special, she might have thought. He's as insensitive as every other man. But his patient love showed that he was different and quickly helped to awaken love in her as well. No sooner had he left her a reminder of his visit than she says, "My feelings were aroused for him. . . . My soul had gone out to him. . . . But he did not answer me." And one problem seemed to lead to another.

Have you ever observed how disharmony in your relationship with a really important person in your life quickly affects other aspects of your life as well? If you are out of sorts with your girl-friend or boyfriend, husband or wife or parent, everything else seems to go wrong too. The king's wife had this same kind of experience when she was separated from him.

When she had previously sought her husband at night, the watchmen of the city had helped her. Now they mistake her for a stealthy criminal sneaking about in the night. No doubt she could have appeared that way with her long shawl draped around her like the secretive cloak of a thief. At any rate, they first arrest her rather harshly before jerking off her shawl and seeing their unlikely suspect, their frustrated queen.

"The watchmen who go about in the city found me. They struck me; they bruised me. They took my shawl from upon me—those guardians of the walls." Her indifferent response had led to dismal circumstance.

Nevertheless, it sometimes takes such an unfortunate circumstance to awaken us to the seriousness of our predicament. For example, sickness may make a person want to mend his relationship with a person against whom he has borne a grudge. Up to then he could have put it out of his mind, but once sick he faces the problem and determines to solve it as soon as he is well.

The misfortune that this woman experienced probably strengthened her determination to be reconciled to her husband. No wonder that immediately after her misfortune she cries out for help from the women of the palace. "I adjure you, O daughters of Jerusalem, if you find my beloved—as to what you will tell him—(tell him) that I am faint with love." She had come a long way from the ingratitude that led to her problem in the first place.

I Won't Last a Day Without You

Every marriage will have problems, but a successful marriage will work through those problems. In this model romance, the problem of indifference on the part of the wife has emerged. This, in turn, however, raised another potential problem on the part of the husband—wounded pride. His masculine pride could have been offended. He may have wished to go off somewhere and pout for a while. But already we have seen her attitude of indifference transformed to appreciation and his potentially wounded pride covered by patient love. Yet they are still apart. However, by their attitudes they are moving towards reconciliation. The next two stanzas of the song introduce two necessary steps toward that reconciliation.

Both steps toward reconciliation are introduced by questions from women in the court, the daughters of Jerusalem. The first question they ask is, "What is your beloved more than another lover?" Her answer to that reveals how much he really means to her. Their second question to her is, "Where has your beloved gone?" Her answer to that reveals his whereabouts and sets the stage for their reunion. The first question prepares her attitude; the second leads to their meeting.

At the root of indifference is ingratitude. Had she really been grateful for her husband, she could not have been indifferent to him. Thus when the daughters of Jerusalem ask their first question, they give the young wife the encouragement and opportunity to remember and express her appreciation of her husband. And she is poetic about that expression.

Daughters of Jerusalem to Bride

5:9　*What is your beloved more than another lover,*
　　O fairest among women?
　　What is your beloved more than another lover,
　　that so you adjure us?

Bride to Daughters of Jerusalem

10　*My beloved is dazzlingly ruddy,*
　　distinguished among ten thousand.
11　*His head is pure gold;*
　　His locks, palm leaves, black as a raven.
12　*His eyes are like doves beside streams of water,*
　　bathed in milk and reposed in their setting.
13　*His cheeks are a bed of balsam, a raised bed of spices.*
　　His lips are lilies, dripping with liquid myrrh.
14　*His hands are cylinders of gold set with jewels.*
　　His abdomen is a plate of ivory covered with sapphires.
15　*His legs are alabaster pillars set upon pedestals*
　　of fine gold.
　　His appearance is like Lebanon, choice as the cedars.
16　*His mouth is sweetness,*
　　And all of him is wonderful.
　　This is my beloved and this is my friend,
　　O daughters of Jerusalem.

She says that he is the best-looking man around, "dazzlingly ruddy, distinguished among ten thousand." He must have had a golden tan and healthy dark hair, for she says that "his head is pure gold; his locks, palm leaves, black as a raven." And when we see that later she says, "His appearance is like Lebanon, choice as the cedars," then we realize that he was really "tall, dark, and hand-some" if ever anyone was. Yet his eyes were soft and tender and clear "like doves beside streams of water, bathed in milk and re-posed in their setting."

Perhaps he wore a fragrant cologne that she always associated with him too. For she remarks that "his cheeks are a bed of balsam, a raised bed of spices." She knew how sweet his kisses were. "His lips are lilies, dripping with liquid myrrh." And he was al-ways ready to place a gentle hand upon her to comfort her, to guide her, or to caress her. She could therefore describe his hands as "cylinders of gold set with jewels."

Yet although he was gentle, he was also very strong both in stat-ure and in character. He certainly wasn't out of shape. She said, "His abdomen is a plate of ivory covered with sapphires." He had rippling stomach muscles that were firm from exercise. "His legs," she said, "are alabaster pillars set upon pedestals of fine gold." He couldn't be shaken when the winds of adversity blew against him. Alabaster pillars wouldn't easily give way.

What a dignity he possessed too! She could describe his overall appearance as "like Lebanon, choice as the cedars." He was an im-pressive young man.

When he spoke he was not crude or crass. On the contrary, he spoke carefully and wisely. And hence his wife can say, "His mouth is sweetness." So full of praise, she is almost exhausted. She can only conclude that "all of him is wonderful. This is my beloved and this is my friend." This wonderful person is not only her lover but her friend and companion for life. Right now some of us are probably asking ourselves how in the world she could have ever been so indifferent to and ungrateful for a man like him. No doubt some wife is now saying that "I could surely see being ungrateful for the rascal I got, but I could never be ungrateful for a man like Solomon."

Yet there was a time when that rascal, and probably most every other husband, was the most wonderful man in the world to his wife. She probably felt like thanking God for him. Yet somewhere along the line the smugness of ingratitude crept in. "I really deserve him and better" or "I really deserve her and better." And then the problems begin to multiply so fast that you lose track. At the base of them all is simple ingratitude. Then that wonderful man or woman may really become unattractive.

How wise it was of the poet of our romance to include one problem which is at the foundation of so many others in marriage. The poet got right to the heart of the matter by getting to the heart of the person. The heart of ingratitude had to be transformed to the heart of appreciation before the reunion could take place. But now since the wife of our song really appreciates her husband, she can proceed in the next step toward reconciliation. Perhaps other wives and husbands should make a list of the reasons why they appreciate each other too.

Run and Find the One Who Loves You

The ability of a couple to succeed in their marriage is equal to the ability of that couple to forgive and accept forgiveness. Notice it is not just the ability to forgive but also the ability to accept forgiveness. One may be willing to forgive but the other unwilling to accept it. That still leaves a broken relationship. When this willingness on the part of both becomes a habit, then the bubble of romance that began their relationship will become a diamond that will last forever.

Bubbles are nice; they rise fast and are lovely in their form; but they lack the beauty and stability of a diamond. And unless the bubble becomes a diamond, it could easily be pricked by wounded pride or ingratitude and then be lost forever, almost forgotten except for the liquid tear it leaves upon the ground.

How does this miraculous transformation take place? Only by forgiveness and its reception—two simple things to say but difficult to do. Yet both were exercised by the lovers of our song. His forgiveness, her reception and a diamond before our eyes—here's how it happened.

Daughters of Jerusalem to Bride

6:1   *Where has your beloved gone, O fairest among women?*
       Where has your beloved turned, that we may
          seek him with you?

Bride to Daughters of Jerusalem

2   *My beloved has gone to his garden, to beds of balsam,*
       to pasture his flock among the gardens
       and to gather lilies.

3   *I am my beloved's and my beloved is mine—the one*
       who pastures his flock among the lilies.

King to Bride

4   *Fair you are, my darling, as Tirzah,*
       lovely as Jerusalem,
       awe-inspiring as bannered hosts.

5   *(Turn your eyes from me for they arouse me.)*
       Your hair is like a flock of goats which descend from Gilead.

6   *Your teeth are like a flock of young lambs,*
       which have come up from the washing,
       all of which are paired,
       and not one among them is alone.

7   *Your temples are like a slice of a pomegranate*
       behind your veil.

8   *There are sixty queens and eighty concubines*
       and maidens without number;

9   *(But) unique is she—my dove, my perfect one;*
       unique is she to her mother;
       pure is she to the one who bore her.

> *The daughters saw her and called her blessed;*
> *The queens and concubines praised her.*

After hearing the queen praise her husband, the women of the court quite understandably ask, "Where has your beloved gone, O fairest among women? Where has your beloved turned, that we may seek him with you?" They want to help her find him and take another look at him for themselves.

This young wife then replies, "My beloved has gone to his garden, to beds of balsam, to pasture his flock among the gardens and to gather lilies. I am my beloved's and my beloved is mine—the one who pastures his flock among the lilies."

From this we can see three important facts which pave the way for forgiveness from her husband. First, she knows where he has gone—probably to his favorite garden. She knows the place where they can be by themselves to talk. Second, even though they are separated, she still knows that they belong to one another. She can still affirm, "I am my beloved's and my beloved is mine." She is secure enough in their relationship to know that she doesn't have to worry about divorce whenever there is a problem.

By the way, this is the great advantage to a marriage commitment where a divorce is not an option. The commitment provides the firm boundaries within which the problems are to be worked out. She knew they had that firm commitment.

But thirdly, she recognizes the attitude of her husband to be gentle and patient though he may have had good reason to be angry. She indicates this recognition by emphasizing the shepherdlike qualities of her husband while he is in the garden. He pastures "his flock among the gardens" and gathers the lilies. She may have pictured him strolling through the garden patiently waiting for her to come to her senses and return to him. Then she emphasizes his patience by repeating the expression "the one who pastures his flock among the lilies." This is the one who is waiting for her.

And he furnishes a good example of one principle often necessary in the resolution of conflicts: Patient silence can often prepare the way for reunion. It allows the dust to settle and the heat to cool. The patient silence on his part gave her time to realize her offense. Then she was ready to receive the forgiveness he was always ready to give.

At last she goes down to the garden. Even though she knew he would forgive her, at the same time she was probably a bit fearful of what he might say. "I really shouldn't have acted that way. But everyone acts that way sometimes. Still, I shouldn't have. I wonder if he's angry. Could he be regretting that he married me? Could he possibly be wishing that he married one of the girls in the palace? I wish I hadn't acted that way." Finally, she meets him face to face.

I Honestly Love You

To her surprise she is met with compliments. Has he forgotten their problem? "Fair you are, my darling, as Tirzah, lovely as Jerusalem, awe-inspiring as bannered hosts." He praises her loveliness and the dignity of her character. Then she lifts her eyes to his, but he gently says, "Turn your eyes from me for they arouse me." Why does he not want to be physically aroused by her? she wonders. Then he goes on to praise her with compliments he has frequently given before. He has previously said to her, "Your hair is like a flock of goats which descend from Gilead." He then praises her lovely smile, "Your teeth are like a flock of young lambs, which have come up from the washing, all of which are paired, and not one among them is alone." Yet he has also said this before. Then he praises her bright healthy cheeks, "Your temples are like a slice of a pomegranate behind your veil." Once again has she not heard this before? Why of course she has. These were the very compliments he had given her on her wedding night! It was his way of telling her that she was still the girl he married, as precious and dear to him now as then.

After their first problem, he does not become angry and say, "Well, you're certainly not the person I thought I was marrying." He tenderly assures her that he loves her as much as ever, and he does so by complimenting her in the same way he did the night they were married.

Yet his praise is not exactly as it was on their wedding night. He omits that praise which is more sensual and sexual in nature. He does not, for example, refer to her lips or breasts as he did then. Nor does he refer to her shapely hips as he later will. Rather he avoids that, and even asks her to turn her eyes from him lest they arouse him. He wants to assure her of his love for her, but very wisely he guards against a possible misconception on her part, the misconception that the only reason he wished to make up with her was so he could make love to her.

Isn't that why many selfish lovers all of a sudden want to be kind to their partners only late in the evening after a day of argument or even total indifference? Was this his reason? He had come to her at night when she had been indifferent to him. Perhaps she might think he wished reconciliation only so that he might not be refused on a later night.

But this was not the case. He wanted to be close to her as a life partner not simply as a sex partner. Sex apart from love would be an empty sham, a pretension that love was being expressed when in reality there was no love to express. First their love relationship had to be mended, then the sexual relationship would take care of itself. And as a matter of fact, this is exactly what happened to them. In the next chapter we will see their tenderest, most intimate sexual experience thus far. But here he assures her of his genuine forgiveness by praising her with the same compliments he had given her on their wedding night, and he carefully avoids the sexual aspects of that praise which might lead her to suspect his motives.

Although he omitted some of those compliments with good reason, he added certain others which are more suited for this reconciliation scene. "There are sixty queens and eighty concubines and maidens without number; (but) unique is she—my dove, my perfect one; unique is she to her mother; pure is she to the one who bore her." He was not regretting that he had married her. He was not wishing that he had married a girl from the palace court. She was as different from them as a "lily among thorns."

He did not go off in a dream world, feel sorry for himself, and wish he had married someone else. Such an attitude, in fact, would only have compounded the problem. Quite the opposite, he very creatively and compassionately assured her of his forgiveness. She was still the girl he married, and he was thankful for her. There was no wounded pride on his part.

Yet surely there was the possibility for it. And if ingratitude is the root of half of the problems in marriage, then pride must be the root of the other half. Potentially, it would have damaged this relationship, but the king in humility refused to allow it.

The poet of this romance has shown himself doubly wise. He has included the two problems of marriage which are at the base of so many other problems. He really got to the root of the matter. Ask yourself this question—if every marriage partner could avoid pride and ingratitude, how many unhappy marriages would there be? How many marriages would be transformed if each partner sought simply to love and serve the other in appreciation and humility? Most marriage counselors would be out of a job.

What the World Needs Now

No, the king did not fall prey to the destructiveness of wounded pride. He did not act in petty revenge; he did not determine to "get back" at his wife. He thought only of assuring her of his forgiveness. Yet forgiveness is a two-way street. She also needed to receive

it. That's what is next described, and with that the bubble has become a diamond before our eyes.

King to Bride

6:10   *"Who is this looking forth like the dawn,*
            fair as the moon,
            pure as the sun,
            awesome as an army with banners?"

Bride in soliloquy

11   *To the garden of nut trees I had gone down*
            to see the fresh shoots of the ravine,
            to see whether the vine had budded or the pomegranates
            had bloomed.

12   *Before I was aware, my soul set me among the chariots*
            of my people, a prince.

Daughters of Jerusalem to Bride

13   *Return, return O Shulamith;*
            Return, return, that we may gaze upon you.

King to Daughters of Jerusalem

        How you gaze upon Shulamith
            as at a dance of Mahanaim!

This section begins with a continuation of the king's praises of his
bride. But here he compliments her in a different sort of way. One
of the best ways to praise someone is to mention the nice things
other people have said about that person. The king is doing this
when he says, "The daughters saw her and called her blessed; the
queens and concubines praised her."

Yet the praise by the daughters of Jerusalem is significant for
another reason too. It happens to be the very praise they gave her
upon seeing the reconciliation of the king and his wife. So when we
look at their praises of his wife, we can discover what happened at
the reconciliation scene from their point of view.

The daughters of Jerusalem praise the loveliness of the king's wife in figures of progressively brighter light. "Who is this looking forth like the dawn, fair as the moon, pure as the sun, awesome as an army with banners?" First she appears as distant and dim as the first light of dawn, then as fair as the moon, and finally as pure as the sun with the awesomeness of an army. She seems to be first at a distance but progressively coming closer to them. Then their next words after the bride speaks seem to indicate that she is departing from them because they say, "Return, return O Shulamith; return, return, that we may gaze upon you." It's as if she were in a race car that first appeared on the horizon, came closer, then whizzed by and off before they could take a good look at her.

Of course, she wasn't in a race car, but she may likely have been in something like it, a chariot. When the bride speaks between the praises of the daughters of Jerusalem, she makes the somewhat puzzling statement, "Before I was aware, my soul set me among the chariots of my people." She evidently really was in a chariot racing by when the daughters of Jerusalem saw her and praised her. How does this shed light on the reconciliation scene? I think we need to look at the significance of the chariots.

You see, King Solomon was famous for his many chariots. Her riding upon his own lead chariot identified her with him again and indicated they were back together. It would be as if a couple in high school broke up and the girl was never seen riding in her boyfriend's famous red, white and blue sports car. Yet when they had gotten back together, everyone knew, for there she was, hair blowing in the wind as she rode down the main drag with him in his sports car. The king's wife was now identified closely with him by similar means.

Actually this interpretation is confirmed by the very significant name she is called by the daughters of Jerusalem when she races by, "Return, return O Shulamith," they say. What does this name mean? In the original language in which this song was written,

"Shulamith" was simply the feminine form of the name Solomon, the name of the king. It would be like "Don and Donna" in our language. The name would thus mean that she was the feminine counterpart of Solomon, his opposite number.

The daughters of Jerusalem thus acknowledge that she and Solomon are now closely identified with one another and that now they are back together. Naturally they want to take a good look at this woman, worthy to be the counterpart of the king. No wonder they cry out for her to return that they may gaze upon her. The king remarks in fact that they loved to gaze upon her as intensely as if they were looking upon a festive dance.

But still we have not considered the reconciliation scene from Shulamith's point of view. How does she remember it? In her typical simplicity she recounts it in a few words. "To the garden of nut trees I had gone down to see the fresh shoots of the ravine, to see whether the vine had budded or the pomegranates had bloomed. Before I was aware, my soul set me among the chariots of my people, a prince."

She went down to the garden because she knew that was where he would be. She poetically gives the reason for her going as being "to see whether the vine had budded or the pomegranates had bloomed." She wanted to know if it would be spring again. Because their relationship had begun in springtime, the coming of a new spring would signify the coming of a new spring in their relationship, a new season of love. It would indicate that their relationship had gone through a full cycle and reached a new plateau. She went down to the garden to see if their reconciliation might bring that new spring.

We know what happened when she went there. She was met with praises from her husband. All she recounts to the daughters of Jerusalem is this, "Before I was aware, my soul set me among the chariots of my people, a prince." Almost before she knew it, they were together again. Naturally she was not aware of the precise moment. By its very nature the reception of forgiveness means seeing yourself as the other person sees you. So at the moment you are forgiven your eyes are off yourself and on another.

Guilt had turned her eyes inward, but he brought them outward. She went down to the garden in self-conscious guilt in the hope of renewal, and she was met with praise which turned her eyes from herself to him, and once to him, back to herself through his eyes of forgiveness. He still saw the woman he loved on his wedding night. That resolved the "communication breakdown" and brought a whole new spring of romance for both of them complete with flowers, gifts and kisses.

New Seasons
of
Spring

True love is,
A love that shall be new and
fresh each hour,
As is the sunset's golden mystery,
Or the sweet coming of the evening star,
Alike, and yet most unlike, every day,
And seeming ever best and fairest now.

James Russell Lowell, "Love"

FIVE

"I never knew what happiness was until I got married, but then it was too late." "Marriage is a great institution, but who wants to spend the rest of his life in an institution." These, of course, are supposed to be jokes, but they all too often reflect a serious truth.

We look around at most marriages today and wonder if it is even possible for a couple to really grow in their love for one another, to experience a deeper and richer love as the seasons pass from one to the next. It seems that genuine excitement and appreciation for each other soon gives way to a boring tolerance of a situation without remedy.

The Creator of marriage certainly did not intend such misery. He did not design this misfortune as a sort of divine penalty for the happiness of the first few months of romance. He is not a master of deceit who loves to trap people in varying degrees of agony dying a slow death chained to their worst enemy. Believe it or not, marriage is really supposed to become better with age.

No one knew that more than the model lover of our song, King

Solomon. He is the same one who wrote the book of Proverbs. And in that book he gave young men some good advice on marriage. "Rejoice in the wife of your youth," he urges. "As a loving hind and a graceful doe, let her breasts satisfy you at all times; be exhilarated always with her love" (5:18-19, NASV). The king heeded his own advice in the song. The new spring of his romance brought a marriage that was deeper and richer in every aspect of their relationship—in their lovemaking, in their conversation, in all their experiences together.

God's Snugglers

A very popular book recently has been *God's Smuggler*, the story of Brother Andrew's efforts to take Bibles behind the Iron Curtain. It is a great service Brother Andrew is doing, and I don't mean to minimize it by the play on the title of his book in this section's subheading. Brother Andrew is bringing glory to God in his service. Yet would you believe that in the very tender lovemaking we are about to see in this song that the couple is also bringing glory to God? And they are doing so in the way that any of God's servants bring glory to Him, by obediently living as God intended.

This couple is obeying God in marriage by being very much in love and very expressive of that love. Not that they should do so at the expense of other responsibilities of course. No one is saying that. But there is a time and place for love, and when it is given, it should be as tender and as meaningful as theirs.

The king wrote in another of his works that there was a time and place for everything, including "a time for embracing" (Eccles. 3:5). This was that time.

King to Bride

7:2   *How beautiful are your feet in sandals, O prince's daughter.*
         The curves of your thighs are like ornaments,
            the work of the hands of an artist.

3   *Your navel is a rounded goblet never lacking mixed wine.*
    Your abdomen is a stack of wheat enclosed with lilies.
4   *Your two breasts are like two fawns, twins of a gazelle.*
5   *Your neck is like a tower of ivory.*
    Your eyes are like the pools in Heshbon
        by the gate of the populous city.
    Your nose is like a tower in Lebanon keeping watch
        over Damascus.
6   *Your head crowns you as Carmel,*
    And the flowing locks of your head are like purple threads.
    The king is held captive by your tresses.
7   *How beautiful and how pleasant you are—love in (your)*
        exquisite delights.
8   *This your stature is comparable to a palm tree,*
        and your breasts to its clusters.
9   *I say, "I will climb the palm tree;*
    I will take hold of its fruit stalks;
    Oh, may your breasts be like clusters of the vine
        and the fragrance of your breath like apples
10 *and your mouth like the best wine..."*

Bride (to King)

    ... going down smoothly for my beloved,
    flowing gently through the lips of the sleeping ones.

The poet has deliberately arranged this account of their lovemaking in the same pattern as he described their wedding night. He first recounts the praise (7:2-8); then he notes the king's declaration of what he shall do (7:9-10). And lastly he records the response by the wife. By arranging the story of this night in that pattern he makes it easy for us to compare the two nights and see what changes may have taken place in their relationship.

   One of the first things we notice is that the praise of the king is much more sensual and intimate. It reflects a greater knowledge of the physical beauty of his wife. For example, here he praises the curves of her thighs and the soft warmth of her stomach. Yet he did not include this on their wedding night. Perhaps he could not for at that point he had no real knowledge of that. But now we can expect a fuller expression and more detailed description of his praise for her.

You Fill Up My Senses

He starts at the bottom of her feet and praises her to the top of her head. First he compliments the loveliness of her feet in sandals. Then he compares the curves of her thighs to "ornaments, the work of the hands of an artist." The curves of the upper part of her thighs included her hips. They were like ornaments because they were so precisely curved and very beautiful. Yet no human artist created those curves. Only the ultimate Creator of all beauty could have done so.

Next he compares her navel to a rounded glass never lacking mixed wine and her abdomen to a stack of wheat enclosed with lilies. Wine and wheat were the basic foods of any meal. His joining these two images in his praise of her stomach must mean that her stomach is like a wonderful feast to him. And it is implicit in his praise that he would kiss her warm stomach as later he expresses the explicit desire to kiss her breasts. It is all a part of their lovemaking, and God does not stutter to describe it.

He describes her breasts as "two fawns, twins of a gazelle." We have seen how as one naturally desires to caress baby deer, so he naturally desired to caress her breasts. When he compares her neck to a tower of ivory, he is probably complimenting not only the noble dignity exemplified in her posture but also the artistic smoothness of her neck. As he gently slid his fingers down her neck it was smooth as ivory to him.

When he looked into her eyes, they were peaceful and gentle. So he compares them to certain well-known pools of water in their land—the pools of Heshbon by the gate of the populous city. And notice how he implicitly contrasts the peaceful pools of water with the busyness of a populous city. What a lovely analogy by which to compliment his wife. A man could draw aside from the haste and hurry of the multitudes to rest by the pools of water by the city gate. So the weary king could leave the business and demands of a responsible position and find serenity as peaceful as unruffled water.

Perhaps he again praises her character when he compares her nose to "a tower in Lebanon keeping watch over Damascus." Damascus was the capital of the Syrians, a frequent enemy of their people. Towers facing toward Damascus would be for protection of the nation. In like manner her stately look perhaps reflected the strong character which was her protection.

Yet the most beautiful aspect of his wife was her lovely face. It crowned her as Mount Carmel crowned the land. As Carmel was beautiful and impressive atop the rich land, so her face was beautiful and impressive atop her exquisite figure, a lovely crown on a lovely queen.

And he loved her luxurious hair. He tells her, "The flowing locks of your head are like purple threads. The king is held captive by your tresses." Purple represents royalty, so she must have the flowing hair of a queen. And what a playful picture he presents when he says, "The king is held captive by your tresses." No chains in the land were strong enough to bind him. Yet as he embraces his wife, he is held captive by the soft threads of her hair draped around him.

This concludes his orderly praise of her from her feet to the top of her head. However, there is one more thing we should observe about his praise this night in comparison to the praise he gave on their wedding night. On that night he praised seven aspects of his bride. And since seven was the number of perfection we realized that even in the number of compliments he gave he was telling her how perfect she was. Only one other number in Scripture is the number of perfection, and that is the number ten. And when we count the number of aspects he praised on this night, we discover precisely that number.

It is a growth in perfection. Perhaps you have heard some couples remark that in comparison to the love they have at the present, the love they had when they were married was really small. Yet they really loved one another when they were married. It is simply that greater knowledge had produced a deeper love. Similarly the couple of our song experienced such growth in their lives. On their wedding night he could give sevenfold praise, but on this later night he could give tenfold praise. Their love had truly deepened.

Yet this deeper love can also be seen in the remainder of their lovemaking. Remember on the wedding night there was the almost formal request and acceptance in the imagery of the garden. It was easily compared to the first kiss of Romeo and Juliet. But notice now how much freer the couple is with one another. It is not a loss in sacredness but rather a growth in familiarity.

Now the king can be so bold as to say, "How beautiful and how pleasant you are—love in (your) exquisite delights. This your stature is comparable to a palm tree, and your breasts to its clusters." He declares that her breasts shall be like the clusters of a vine. And thus he creates a vivid picture of his kissing her breasts as one would place the clusters of the vine to one's lips. And her kisses would bring the fragrance of her breath like the sweet scent of apples, and her mouth would be "like the best wine" to be slowly and exquisitely enjoyed with every sip. This is a different mood from the delicate formality of their wedding night.

And whereas the bride made an almost formal reply on their wedding night, here she can fluidly interrupt and finish the sentence of the king. He says, "Your mouth like the best wine . . ."; she concludes, ". . . going down smoothly for my beloved, flowing gently through the lips of the sleeping ones." And with that the lovemaking is over.

But what about the passion of consummation? Why has the poet passed over that and simply concluded with the lovers falling asleep? It is because he has a lesson to teach. Whereas the wedding night focused on the purpose of sex as the consummation of marriage, this night focuses on the purpose of sex as the nourishment of marriage. The former concluded that consummation had taken place; the latter, that the effect of consummation had been the closeness of a couple falling asleep in each other's arms.

As they fell asleep the last kiss lingered in each other's minds like the aftertaste of good wine. What an enchanting picture of the sleeping couple! Their sexual expression of love truly served its purpose in their lives. It both consummated their love and nourished it as well.

Paradise Regained

The richness of that nourishment can be seen in the statement of the wife on the following morning, "I am my beloved's and his desire is for me." It is a brief statement and therefore easy to overlook its profound significance. This statement has been slightly but carefully changed from its previous two usages. Altogether its three occurrences are as follows: "My beloved is mine and I am his" (2:16); "I am my beloved's and my beloved is mine" (6:3); "I am my beloved's and his desire is for me" (7:11).

Notice how the woman's security in her husband's love has deepened. When the wife first utters this refrain she places her possession of the beloved primary, and his possession of her secondary. Yet the second time she reverses that, placing his possession of her primary, which would indicate her greater measure of security in him. Yet after the experience of 7:2-10 she not only places his possession of her primary, but strengthens it by adding that his desire is toward her, and so focused is she upon him that she omits her possession of him. She has really lost herself in him and thereby found herself.

But furthermore, the word in the original language translated "desire" in "his desire is for me" is very carefully chosen. It is used only twice elsewhere in Scripture. One of those occurrences, quite significantly, is in Genesis 3:16 where part of the curse on mankind would be the woman's excessive, perhaps unreturned, desire toward her husband. But in this romance the husband's desire is just as strong toward his wife. It is almost as if the Scriptures were saying that in a truly ideal marriage part of the curse on mankind is reversed.

In this chapter we have seen the growth of their ideal marriage in many ways. In the sensuous more knowledgeable praise, the bolder initiation and more passionate description of his caresses, in the smoother more fluid response of the wife, and in the fulfillment of the enriching purposes of sex—in all these ways these verses have demonstrated a progression in the maturity of their relationship together. And it illustrates no loss of sacredness but a growth in familiarity and freedom.

Morning Has Broken Like the First Morning

The freedom of the wife continues to grow however. It can be seen in the next verses which record the wife's invitation to her husband to go to the country where she will give her caresses to him (7:13).

7:12   *Come, my beloved, let us go out into the country.*
         Let us spend the night in the villages.

13   *Let us rise early to the vineyards.*
         Let us see whether the vine has budded
             and its blossoms have opened
             and whether the pomegranates have bloomed.
         There I will give my caresses to you.

14   *The mandrakes have given forth fragrance*
and over our doors are all choice fruits—
both new and old, which I have stored up for
you, my beloved.

Psychologists have observed that in a maturing marriage the wife feels the necessary freedom to initiate lovemaking more frequently as the marriage relationship grows. Perhaps that is the case here. For this is the first time she has done so, and it does follow her proclamation of security in her husband's love.

But even within the verses themselves are indications that they have reached a new plateau in their relationship. Notice that she longs to see "whether the vine has budded and its blossoms have opened." The possibility of spring flowers just blooming discloses the time of year—the transition from winter to spring. It is about to be spring again. And yet they courted and were wed in mid-spring (2:10-14). The poet thus reveals that their relationship has gone from spring to spring, that now it has experienced a full cycle of growth.

In the new spring the time is right for love. "The mandrakes have given forth fragrance and over our doors are all choice fruits—both new and old, which I have stored up for you, my beloved." In the ancient world the mandrake plant was considered to possess aphrodisiac qualities. So the wife says in effect that the atmosphere is conducive to their expressions of love.

Yet the cycle of growth is reemphasized by the description of the fruits she has saved for her husband—"new" and "old." "New" probably refers to the fresh fruits of the new spring, "old," to the dried fruits of the previous spring. So she intends to give her love in qualities new and old: both freshly and creatively and yet in ways familiar and memorable.

The nature of love is to be constant in its manners of expression, yet always fresh and refreshing as spring. In initiating the giving of this love in the new spring of their relationship, the wife has disclosed once again the development of her marriage.

You Are the Sunshine of My Life

Marriage is not really a single relationship. It is a composition of many relationships. Your partner is lover, friend, teacher, student, brother or sister and child all in one person. And the better the marriage the more evident is every aspect. In our model romance in its maturity each of these facets becomes sparklingly clear. And the brightness of each facet illumines the fullness of that relationship.

Bride to King

8:1   *Oh that you were like a brother to me*
      who nursed at the breasts of my mother.
    If I found you outdoors I would kiss you,
      and no one would despise me either.

2   *I would lead you;*
    I would bring you to the house of my mother.
    You would instruct me.
    I would give you spiced wine to drink, the nectar
      of my pomegranate.

3   *Oh may his left hand be under my head and his right hand*
      embrace me.

to Daughters of Jerusalem

4   *I adjure you, O daughters of Jerusalem,*
      not to arouse, not to awaken love until it pleases.

First she wishes that he were like a natural brother so that if she found him outside she could kiss him. In their culture it was not proper to express affection publicly to a lover but only to members of the family. For clarity she adds, "who nursed at the breasts of my mother." This makes it certain that she refers to a real brother. She is not using "brother" in the sense of "husband" as he used the term "sister" to refer to his wife. No one would look down on her if she kissed her real brother outside.

Then she seems to wish he were not merely her brother but her younger brother. Notice she says to him, "I would lead you; I would bring you to the house of my mother. You would instruct me." The word translated "lead" always referred to a superior leading an inferior: a general, his army; a king, his captain; a shepherd, his sheep. The king's wife is playfully assuming the role of older sister. She would lead her younger brother to their common home.

Yet, in irony, the one whom she would lead is the one who would teach her. The freedom in their relationship is thus displayed in her playful show of authority over him which quickly gives way to her recognition of his leadership over her. As her beloved teacher she would give him spiced wine to drink from her pomegranate, the ancient version of the apple for the teacher.

But he is not only her teacher. He is also her husband and lover. Thus she can wish, "Oh may his left hand be under my head and his right hand embrace me." She longed to be caressed by her wonderful husband. So in just three short verses we see that she knew her husband as brother, teacher and lover. We have already seen that she knew him as her friend as well. Yet he is one husband. They completed one another in every respect. Each needed friendship, love, instruction and the security of a family. Each found all of this in the other. And as she quickly moves from one facet of the relationship to the next, it is like the slight movement of a diamond in the light, shimmering off every facet of its brilliance. The fullness of their relationship could not be more exquisitely displayed.

In every way we have seen a marriage in maturity. In their more intimate sexual experience, in the greater security of the wife, in her playful freedom to initiate love, and finally in the fullness of their relationship the poet has sketched a revealing portrait of this model couple.

No wonder his wife now says once again, "I adjure you, O daughters of Jerusalem, not to arouse, not to awaken love until it pleases." The reader having just seen their lovely portrait of marriage might be tempted more than ever to force such a relationship in impatience.

VI
The Nature
of
Love

My bounty is as boundless
as the sea,
my love as deep.
The more I give to thee,
the more I have,
for both are infinite.

William Shakespeare,
Romeo and Juliet

SIX

Charlie Brown says love is a warm puppy. Ali McGraw says love means never having to say you're sorry. The cartoons say that love is cleaning his whiskers out of the basin, having each other when bad news is received, waiting up to see if he comes home safely and laughing at old baby photos. I suppose all of these definitions contain a measure of truth. But when this song for lovers gave its definition of love there were more than cartoons and warm puppies.

First the poet sets the couple before us who had experienced the heights and depths of romantic love. Then in the climactic peak of his song he tells us what love is really all about. And he does it in the following verses.

Poet

8:5   *Who is this coming from the wilderness, leaning*
       on her beloved?

Bride to King

    Beneath the apple tree I awakened you;
      there your mother was in labor with you;

> *there she was in labor and gave you birth.*
6   *Put me as a seal upon your heart,*
> *As a seal upon your arm.*
> *For strong as death is love.*
> *Relentless as Sheol is jealousy.*
> *Its flashes are flashes of fire,*
>   *the flame of Yahweh.*
7   *Many waters cannot extinguish this love*
>   *and rivers will not drown it.*
> *If a man were to give all the possessions of his house*
>   *for love, he would be utterly despised.*

A Portrait of Their Love

Before he gives his definition of love he sets before the reader a picture of the couple who had experienced it in their relationship. The picture was taken after their second honeymoon in the country. Off in the distance they can be seen strolling together. Her head is gently leaning upon his chest and his arm is around her. "Who is this coming from the wilderness, leaning on her beloved?" the poet asks, and in asking he draws our attention to the lovers of our song. What will he say are the characteristics of love?

The Sweetheart Tree

Actually the poet gives his definition in the form of a statement and a request by the king's young wife. Her initial statement is puzzling at first: "Beneath the apple tree I awakened you; there your mother was in labor with you; there she was in labor and gave you birth." What does she mean by this? The first clue is the phrase, "I awakened you." Three times in the song we have heard the advice, "not to arouse, not to awaken love until it pleases," and its last occurrence was in the verse just preceding this one. Evidently love was pleased to awaken under the apple tree because she awakened him. She awakened his love at a particular time.

But why did love please to awaken at this time? It is because they were under an apple tree but not a literal one. The apple tree was a familiar symbol for romance in their culture. It was the sweetheart tree of the ancient world. The circumstances were favorable; the atmosphere was right. And when the time was right their love began.

Perhaps it is good she is not more specific because the time for romance is different for different people. Some think it is only for the young. But certain older folks with smiles on their faces know that's not true. Nevertheless there is a right time, and when it comes romance begins.

Their love was born where years earlier he himself had been born. Not under a literal apple tree but under a symbolic tree of romance. Astrologers tell us that the stars we are born under determine our destiny. But the poet is telling us that the tree Solomon is born under declares his destiny. He was a man favored by God and destined to find fulfillment under the tree of love.

Notice, however, the implicit comparison with the pain of labor preceding birth. The poet points out that his mother had experienced pain when he was born. How did the birth of their romance bring pain? I think it is like this. Solomon's wife had experienced the pain of insecurity and inferiority when they first met. She had not been able to take care of herself as she worked in the vineyards. And it is normal for the humble pain of unworthiness to come upon any two people when they fall in love. Then later in courtship she experienced the pain of longing and the fear of unfulfilled love when they were apart. After marriage she experienced the pain of separation during a conflict in their marriage. Yet here in the analogy one is wonderfully reminded that although there was pain, it was the fruitful pain of birth, the birth of their relationship. So point one in the definition of love is this: Love is painful.

No doubt many of you have felt the sweet pain of longing when the one you love is gone. You have felt the bitter pain of disappointment in an apathetic response. You have experienced the misery of argument and misunderstandings. It is all a part of romantic love, part of the price tag.

Yet it is often a fruitful pain. Last summer my brother Joe left town for a week, and both he and his girlfriend Lucy realized how much they meant to one another. Now she is my sister-in-law. The pains of separation were the birthpangs of their marriage. But even the pain of conflict can bring a deeper understanding and a more meaningful relationship too. Love is painful.

Love Is Surrender

Then Shulamith made the following request: "Put me as a seal upon your heart, as a seal upon your arm. For strong as death is love. Relentless as Sheol is jealousy. Its flashes are flashes of fire, the flame of Yahweh." What does she mean when she wishes to be a seal upon his heart and arm? She gives the justification for her request in what follows. "For strong as death is love." She wishes to be upon his arm because it is the source of his strength. And because it is love that is strong, she wishes also to be upon his heart. That is the source of his affections. Yet she likened the strength of his love to death. It must be because death is like a victorious hero who conquers all in his path. Love, too, will overcome its opposition. But death is also irreversible. And as one cannot reverse death, neither can one reverse this love.

But why does she wish to be as a seal upon his heart and arm? The seal was the signature of the owner with which he identified all his possessions. Does she wish to be imprinted on all his possessions? No, that is probably not the point of comparison.

Frequently in the Old Testament the seal was figuratively used to represent something of great value and hence something from which one would never part. For example, the Lord tells one leader that in the day of reward he would be made like a seal to him (Hag. 2:23). He would be very valuable to him. Or again the Lord threatens one king saying that even if he were a seal on his right hand, he would throw him off (Jer. 22:24). This figure of speech assumes that one would rarely part from his valuable seal. A seal was a possession jealously guarded.

Because she experienced her husband's jealous concern for her, she could wish to be a seal upon his heart. That precious possession upon his heart would represent what she was to him—someone very special from whom he would never part. So she explains her request to be a seal by saying, "Relentless as Sheol is jealousy." Sheol was the place of the dead. And as Sheol would not give up its dead, so the lover would not give up the one loved. This jealousy is just the opposite of indifference and will never allow the one loved to pursue a wayward path unchecked. So point two in our definition of love is this: Love is possessive, not immaturely so, but in the sense of being intensely concerned for the one who is loved. Love is painful; love is possessive.

When you really love a person, you are jealously concerned for his well-being and happiness. You frequently hear people say that loving another is letting him do anything he wants to do. There is an element of truth in that because love must be freely given. You cannot disallow a person to reject you. But that's not the same thing as saying you would let him do anything he wants. No loving mother allows her child to play in a dangerous street. She is jealously concerned for his safety. When you love someone, you are concerned for him. You won't let him harm himself if at all possible. Anything less is not love but indifference.

What an illustration of this kind of love was my roommate in college! He used to be the soundest sleeper I ever knew. Four alarm clocks wouldn't budge him. No doubt he developed this capacity over many years to overcome his own snoring which sounded like a bull elephant. We used to test his ability by turning up the Beatles so loud that the room would shake; nevertheless, this was only slightly above his snoring, and it could not wake him up. When his fiancée heard of this, she was alarmed because she was so light a sleeper that she woke up at the slightest creak. Yet the most amazing thing happened when they got married. He became the world's lightest sleeper and woke up with club in hand at the slightest noise, ready, even anxious, to go to battle for his little woman. Meanwhile she began to sleep like a rock. She had to do so in order to be able to sleep while the human airhorn blasted away at night.

The explanation of the transformation was simple. She felt secure in his loving protection—great warrior that he was. And he assumed the responsibility for her. I suppose there are other ways of testing the security of your wife than by measuring the peacefulness of her sleep. But that may not be a bad place to start. If your love for your wife is possessive—that is, protective and concerned —you can rest assured that it will be evident in her response of security.

If Ever I Would Leave You

This kind of concern is the godly jealousy spoken of in the Bible. It is the burning attitude of love that God has toward his people, frequently manifesting itself as flames of fire. Not unexpectedly, then, the king's wife expands upon her husband's jealous concern in the imagery of fire. The flashes of his burning concern, she says, are "flashes of fire, the flame of Yahweh." The intensity and eternity of his jealous concern for his wife is the same quality as the Lord's for his people. Nothing can extinguish it once it has begun. "Many waters cannot extinguish this love and rivers will not drown it."

Notice she does not say no rivers and waters will come, but that no waters and rivers will overcome it. It is a waterproof torch. Run a river across it, and it is still burning when the waters have passed.

The strength of his love is that great for his precious wife. So point three in this definition of love is this: Love is persevering. It will persevere through the waters of adversity in marriage. Love is painful, possessive and persevering.

Occasionally people speak of a new girlfriend or boyfriend or even a new wife or husband as "the latest flame." Of course, this assumes there were a few other flames in the past or else this wouldn't be the latest one. Evidently either the waters quenched their flames, or they were so weak they burned out of their own accord. Real love isn't like this though. The love on which a beautiful love is built is a persevering flame burning as brightly at the beginning as it does later on.

Once there was a leader in a community whose wife left him to enjoy life as a "free woman." Everything was great for a while, but she soon became so loose she was living like a prostitute. It hardly seemed possible, but eventually this sparkling socialite was so degraded that even all her not-too-choosy lovers would have nothing to do with her.

She decided she didn't have anything to lose by going back to her husband. And though she didn't understand why, she found his flame of love still burning for her. He took her back and forgave her. He clothed her and gave her a firm roof over her head and carved out a place in his house for her once again. Eventually, she was physically and emotionally restored as a healthy and happy wife. That's persevering love. And this story was such a good example of it that it was included in the Bible itself. You can read about it in the book of the prophet Hosea.

No Cash, Credit or Checks Allowed

"Money can't buy me love" was frequently sung on the radio a few years back. The singer was right on target. And, in fact, the poet of our song concludes his definition of love with a similar point. "If a man were to give all the possessions of his house for love, he would be utterly despised."

Why would the man be despised? Is it simply because he has underestimated the price of love? Was it because love is worth a billion dollars and his house worth only a few thousand, so he had made an irresponsible economic judgment? No. He would be despised for reducing love and the person from which it comes to an object. If you set the price of love at a billion dollars, you would reduce it to nothing. By its very nature love must be given. Sex can be bought; love must be given.

The attempt to buy a person's love is an attempt to reduce that person to an object, to deny him that which makes him a person in the image of God—his voluntary choice of the one whom he will love. So if a man offered a girl all the wealth of his house for love, it would be a great insult. It would be an attempt to depersonalize her. For her to accept would be her greatest degradation, and in reality it would almost be legalized prostitution. Personhood precedes love. In depersonalizing, we destroy it. Love is not an object to be bought because it is priceless. And that is the last point in this definition of love.

Love is not only painful, possessive and persevering. It is also priceless. It is priceless because the one who is loved is priceless.

VII
Before the Bells Toll

And hopes, and fears that kindle hope,
An undistinguishable throng,
And gentle wishes long subdued,
Subdued and cherished long!
Samuel Taylor Coleridge, "Love"

SEVEN

The song gave an illuminating definition of love in the last chapter. And the couple of the song provided an excellent example of love in all the chapters preceding. But in a way it would be almost frustrating to end the definition of love by saying all the money in the world couldn't buy it. Most of us probably knew that already. After seeing the end of the wonderful relationship of the song, we'd like to know the right way to find love, not the sure way to lose it.

How did this couple find themselves in the most meaningful relationship of their lives? How did they prepare themselves for it, and how did they meet? That's what we'd like to ask. And that's just what the poet was waiting for us to ask. In the last few verses of the song he flashes back before the spring of courtship to answer these important questions.

A Family That Cared

The most difficult obstacle to growing up has got to be parents. They're always telling you what to do and when to do it. And it seems you can never do exactly what they say. It's a wonder a person ever makes it. Or so we think until we're old enough to appreciate what they've really done.

I remember the football player who was running like crazy, exhilarated and accelerated as he was about to score a touchdown. The only problem was that he was running the wrong way and about to score for the opposite team. At last his frantically running teammates caught up with him, tackled him and prevented his embarrassing accomplishment. But he did not know it. He jumped up angry and yelling and asking what in the world they thought they were doing. Then he looked around and saw what he had nearly done. Silence. "Must have got turned around somehow," he muttered. "Still, they didn't have to tackle so hard," he thought, "but it's a good thing they got me." Sometimes discipline is necessary. And we ought to thank the ones who care enough about us to discipline us as we grow up.

It's great, too, when someone loves us enough to really encourage us when we're doing right. When no one else would care at all what we do, they're smiling and congratulating us when we do a few things right. Really that's what parents are all about, and sometimes older brothers and sisters too. They're trying the best they can to keep us running the right way—kind of like coaches who care for their players.

The first thing the girl of our love song had in her favor was a family that cared enough about her to discipline her and encourage her in the right direction. In her family the older brothers took charge in encouraging her, perhaps because her father passed away. We see their caring attitude in the following verses.

8:8 *We have a little sister and she has no breasts.*
What shall we do for our sister for the day on which
she is spoken for?

9 *If she is a wall,*

we shall build on her a battlement of silver,
But if she is a door,
    we shall enclose her with planks of cedar.

The poet flashes back to a meaningful strategy session held by her brothers when she was a young girl. "We have a little sister and she has no breasts." They recognized they had a responsibility for their little sister who was still in childhood. We know she hasn't reached her teens yet because "she has no breasts." Her brothers want to be prepared early though, so they're planning ahead. They ask themselves what they should do "for the day on which she is spoken for." That refers to her wedding and marriage. What shall they do to prepare her for it?

They devise a simple but effective formula for success. If she is a wall they will "build on her a battlement of silver." That means that if she is virtuous and firm against boys' advances, they'll reward her, trying to improve on what already is good. In the same way a battlement of silver would increase the beauty of a wall, they would try to increase the beauty of her character.

Yet if she is a door they would enclose her with planks of cedar. In other words, if she is as open as a door to advances, they would have to be stricter with her to prevent her hurting herself for marriage. If she could handle responsibility, they would give it to her; but if not, she would be restricted.

Both aspects of that strategy were really necessary. It was like placing a pitchfork behind her and an ice cream cone in front of her to encourage her to go in the right direction. The ice cream cone should have been enough to direct her but in case it wasn't, the pitchfork was always there to redirect her. It was a simple formula all right but much easier to say than to do. Discipline and encouragement take the kind of time that only love will give. But they loved her enough to do it. They loved her enough to do their part in preparing her for marriage.

When I Fall in Love It Will Be Forever

Nevertheless, she did her part as well. Sure they would have been strict with her if she had tended to be promiscuous, but it would have been much better for her and more pleasing to them if she really wanted to prepare herself for marriage too. Otherwise, when she had the opportunity to cut loose, she would have, and they couldn't have prevented it. But she wanted to be the right kind of person for her husband when it came time for marriage. We see all this in her one brief statement: "I was a wall and my breasts were like towers."

Her brothers didn't have to plank up a door. She herself had chosen to be a wall. And finally she grew up. Her breasts were like towers. The towers were the fortresses of the land. They inspired a somber appreciation from the citizens and a healthy respect from their enemies. So she means her breasts were impressive in the same way. Men looked at this good-looking young woman with an acknowledged respect. "She was," they affirmed almost reverently, "a fine looking woman." Her respect for herself brought the same respect from others.

We Belong Together

Her next words are very important. Right after telling us that she has reached the age and maturity for marriage, she tells us, "*Then* I became in his eyes as one who finds peace." To whose eyes is she referring? Whose are "his" eyes? The next verse tells us, "a vineyard belonged to Solomon." He is the one to whom she is referring.

But what does she mean by the expression, "I became in his eyes as one who finds peace"? Actually, she has ever so slightly changed a familiar expression often used in Scripture: "To find grace in one's eyes." And this familiar expression often refers to finding favor before someone.

For example, the Scripture says that "Noah found grace in the eyes of the Lord." But frequently, as in this case, it refers to a girl finding love in the eyes of a man. She is said to have found grace in his eyes. So when this young girl says she has found peace in his eyes, she is saying she has found romance in Solomon's eyes.

You may wonder why she would change the normal expression to finding "peace." Would you believe she has simply made a pun in the original language in which she spoke? Her own name in the song has been Shulamith, and that is the way it sounds in the original language. Solomon's name in the original language sounds like "Shulamoh." And "peace" in the original language is the word "shalom." She says that she, Shulamith, found "shalom" in finding "Shulamoh." She found romance when she found Solomon.

Let's suppose a boy found real giving and sharing in life when he met a girl named Sharon. He could make the pun, "I have found sharing in Sharon." That's the kind of pun Solomon's wife makes.

Although it is a pun she makes, it is a profound one. In the same way that the boy who says he found "sharing in Sharon" says more than that he just found romance, Shulamith says more in saying she found peace in Solomon. She found romance, but beyond that she found the peace and well-being that comes from a happy marriage relationship. She could rest in him.

The First Time Ever I Saw Your Face

Notice carefully the "then" which begins the statement, "Then I became in his eyes as one who finds peace." That word is very emphatic in the original language. It sets the stage for the next verses to reveal when she did find romance with Solomon.

Bride (to all)

8:10 *I was a wall and my breasts were like towers.*
   Then I became in his eyes as one who finds peace.

11 *A vineyard belonged to Solomon at Baal Hamon.*
   He gave the vineyard to caretakers; each one was to bring
      a thousand shekels of silver for its fruit.
12 *My own vineyard belongs to me.*
to King
      The thousand are for you, O Solomon,
         and two hundred for the caretakers of the fruit.

Somehow or another their meeting must be related to Solomon's vineyard at a place called Baal Hamon. It was a vineyard he had rented to caretakers. How are we supposed to know how they met just from this vineyard leased to caretakers? We must think back ... but of course, at the very beginning of their courtship, just as she was brought to the palace she mentions the vineyards. What did she say? It was, "The sun has scorched me. My mother's sons were angry with me. They appointed me caretaker of the vineyards, but of my own vineyard—which belongs to me—I have not taken care."

Evidently her brothers were the caretakers to whom Solomon had rented his vineyard at Baal Hamon. For some reason, perhaps laziness, they passed the responsibility to their sister. So there she was in a miserable situation. At a time when other girls might be out meeting boys, she was out working in some vineyard her brothers had leased and were tired of farming.

But as fortune had it, this wasn't just "some vineyard." This was the king's property. And like any concerned real estate man he periodically looked over his land and its tenants. One day he passed by this particular vineyard. And then he realized this wasn't just "some vineyard" either. The scenery was astonishingly improved! He did a doubletake on the girl out there, and it was then that she became in his eyes as one who finds peace. Soon she passed from work in the heat of the sun to rest in the shadow of the king.

What a great lesson this is! Out in the heat of the sun working long hours she might have thought she would never find a husband. The circumstances certainly didn't make it likely. Yet even in these circumstances the One who ultimately guides the paths of all would cause their paths to cross. Not only did she and her family care about the future and not only was there a man who would care, but God cared too—and long before she or her family or Solomon ever thought to care. No wonder the Scripture says to "cast all your cares on him for he cares for you" (I Pet. 5:7).

Perhaps the realization of God's care over her enabled her to have the attitude revealed in the analogy from caretaking. The caretaker's normal practice was to labor on another's land, promising to give the majority of the profit to the owner with a percentage for himself. In this particular instance the caretaker was responsible to render a thousand shekels to the owner in return for wages of two hundred.

In Shulamith's analogy she states, "My own vineyard belongs to me." Her own vineyard represents her own person (1:6; 2:15). Its "position" before her emphasizes that she is under her free direction to do with herself as she pleases.

And what does she do with herself? She freely gives the value of her own person to her husband, "The thousand are for you, O Solomon." It is as if she says, "Now I am your vineyard, my lover, and I gladly give the entire thousand dollars of my worth to you; I give myself completely, withholding nothing of my trust, my thoughts, my care, my love."

But she also adds, "and two hundred for the caretakers of the fruit." Since in the analogy she is the vineyard, the keepers of the vineyard's fruit must be her brothers who disciplined and encouraged her. She is therefore asking that they be remembered and appreciated. Or to paraphrase it, "Let us not forget that two hundred dollars belong to the ones who took care of the fruit of my vineyard for you. How thankful we must both be to everyone in my family who helped prepare me and protect me for you!"

Although her brothers may have unfairly placed her in the vineyard to work, she does not bear a grudge against them. Perhaps she could say to them what Joseph said to his brothers who mistreated him, "You meant it for evil, but God meant it for good" (Gen. 50:20). For she, like Joseph, ultimately prospered from the mistreatment. Thusly trusting in the purposes of God, she was free from the anxiety of vengeance and free to love them in sincerity.

She was, of course, also free to love her husband from a pure heart. And the continual excitement of that love is reflected in the last words of the song. They are like the last notes of a symphony, re-echoing a significant previous theme. And the theme re-echoed here is the peak of excitement in courtship.

We've Only Just Begun

What I mean is this. The last words of the husband are, "O you who dwell in the gardens, (my) companions are listening for your voice. Let me hear it" (8:13). These are like the words he whispered to his wife during the highest point of their courtship (2:14). Then he had compared his wife to a dove hidden from him, a gentle dove whose voice he wished to hear to learn of the hidden person of her heart. How remarkable that at the end of the song the husband still longs with the same intensity of courtship to grow in the knowledge of his fascinating wife.

And no less remarkable are the last words of his wife. "Hurry, my beloved, and be like a gazelle or a young stag on the mountains of spices" (8:14). Shortly before they were married, she had whispered the delicate request for him to take her as his bride and enjoy her perfumed breasts (2:17; 4:6). Now even at the end of this song in the maturity of marriage she longs with the intensity of courtship to make love to her beloved husband.

Their joy with one another was continually overflowing and fulfilling the design of their Creator. For he himself had clearly told them, "Rejoice in the wife of your youth. As a loving hind and a graceful doe, let her breasts satisfy you at all times; be exhilarated always with her love" (Prov. 5:18-19, NASV).

So the last words of the couple remind us that the fresh romance of their courtship had continued in the fresh romance of their marriage.

VIII

Faith,
Hope
and Therapy

And should any of you desire to attain
to an understanding of the things
which he reads, let him love.
For it is useless for him who loves not,
to attempt to read or to listen to this
Canticle of love, because the
"ignited" word can obtain no lodgment
in a heart that is cold and frozen.

St. Bernard, "Sermon 79"

EIGHT

As we behold the bride of our song we cannot help but admire her. And perhaps we are awakened anew to the freshness and beauty of virtue by her example. She is a spring garden kept for her husband. She is pure water flowing down a mountain stream. It is lovely imagery describing a lovely person. And it is very inspirational. But it can be very discouraging too.

Where Have All the Flowers Gone?

I remember once after I spoke on this song a boy came to me very dejected. "What's the matter?" I asked. "Didn't you like the song?" "Yeah," he said. "I liked it very much. In fact, I liked it so much it depresses me. I see how good this all could be, but when I look at myself I think it's impossible. I'm not the same kind of person as the king, and I've done plenty of things to prove it. I'm not patient or sensitive, and besides all that... well, I've already given up my own purity."

On more than one occasion a girl has come to me with her eyes down, waiting for others to leave so she could ask me something. "What if you really haven't done such a good job preparing yourself for marriage? I mean, it was great for that girl since she had kept herself for her husband. Like you said, her garden was locked to everyone until she was married. To be honest, my garden is in pretty much disorder. What about me?"

A New Garden

Perhaps the answer to this kind of question is best expressed in the imagery of a garden itself. As I said to one particular girl, "If I were a gardener and someone had broken into my garden and overturned the flowers and fairly well spoiled it, I suppose I would be the best person to go in and fix it and place things back like I wanted them. I could accept the problem and restore the garden to its original beauty." What was I implying, she asked.

"Just this," I said. "You are the garden of your Creator. He is the one who made you and he knows how you are best prepared for marriage. He can accept the problem and remake the garden." I was able to say this to that girl because the Creator of life and beauty himself had already said it to another troubled woman many centuries before.

The great one called the Christ once encountered a woman who had just been caught in adultery. Her garden was undoubtedly in disorder. Actually the woman had been selfishly used by the religious leaders to trap Jesus with a question. They had caught her in the act of adultery to bring her to him as a test case. They likely designed the entire occasion since the guilty man evidently went free. But having seized her, they dragged her without pity to the Master and threw her at his feet.

There she lay in embarrassment and dishonor. She bowed her head in shame as a flower bows with a broken stem. And the wilted petals of her face knew only the dew of tears. Yet no compassion came from her callous accusers, no word of encouragement from those who would trap Jesus as well.

"The law says stone her," they growled, "but what do you say we should do?" And they meant, "You're supposed to be so compassionate and loving; are you going to violate the law and forbid us to stone her?"

But do you know what Jesus did? He calmly stooped to the ground and wrote in the sand. He did not look at the woman, perhaps because the pure look in his eyes would only have pierced her heart with deeper shame. He had genuine compassion for this person. So first he dismissed the crowd with one decisive statement: "He who is without sin among you, let him be the first to throw a stone at her." Then beginning with the oldest, they left.

Only he and the woman remained. "Where are they?" He asked. "Did no one condemn you?"

"No one, Lord," she replied.

"Neither do I condemn you," he said. "Go your way and from now on sin no more."

As she slowly raised her head, she looked into the gentle eyes of one she knew spoke truth. And as she realized her forgiveness, her face began to brighten with new hope. Perhaps she bowed her head again, not in shame, but in worship.

The great one, so they had written, was full of grace and truth. In this story we see why. In truth he recognized her past sin and her future need to avoid it. In grace he forgave her and brought her a new beginning. The Lord Jesus had not violated the law; he had overcome it with a higher law of forgiveness. He had accepted the broken flowers of her life and had forgiven them. And then he gave instructions for her part in the restoration of her garden. His forgiveness brought life. Her future obedience would bring restoration—both in healing the emotional scars of the past and in enriching her new life from God.

For Once in My Life

The prospect of restoration is fascinating and mysterious. The mystery of it is like the mystery of spring—full of wonder and joy over the color and song of life. Who can fully understand it? Certainly not us, but perhaps we can see it from another perspective if we view it through another image of the virtue of the bride.

Her virtue was likened to a pure mountain stream and the wells of life-giving water it provided. But, unfortunately, when compared to such an image, many of us perceive our own impurity in thought and action. Where does restoration begin on an impure well?

Imagine, for example, that dirt was seeping through the cracks of a well's inner barriers and polluting the water. Only muddy water could be drawn from this well. Perhaps its owner could dilute his impure water by adding pure water to it. But, on second thought, pure water was doubtfully at hand since he likely owned but one well. And, after all, even if pure water were available, the diluted water would still be impure from the dirt.

Really, a new well was the only solution—or, more precisely, a maker of new wells. But this is also the solution to the well of an impure heart. And incredible as it may sound at first, the making of new wells is one of the chief occupations of the carpenter from Nazareth.

He does not mock us by asking us to purify ourselves. He knows it is useless to mix the fresh water of "good deeds" with the muddy water of our lives. How in the first place could we draw fresh water from an impure well? And even if one could, would not the diluted water still be impure? Yes, and that is why he must make a new well. Then from the well of a new heart may flow the fresh water of virtue springing from obedience to its Maker.

But once again we know this to be true only because we have heard him explain this before. He was resting on a well, in fact, when he did. The sun was hot that day; its rays caused his sweat-covered face to glisten brightly. His squinting eyes saw the lone figure of a woman approaching on the horizon, slowly journeying through the waves of heat rising from the desert sand. She likely came at this time every day when no one else was present. For, you see, she was an outcast of society who journeyed through much of life alone.

She had been married five times and was presently living with another man. She had tried to drink at the fountain of romance but had been drinking from a forbidden well. It had been like drinking salt water—the more she drank the more thirsty she became. Now she was an outcast making her daily trek to the well. But today she would hear of a well that would finally satisfy her thirst.

After initiating conversation with her by asking her for a drink, Jesus made a startling claim. "If you knew the gift of God," he said, "and who it is who says to you, 'Give me a drink,' you would have asked Him and He would have given you living water." She needed only to know the gift and the giver to receive the gift of living water. It was hers for the asking. And what a gift it was—no less than eternal life that satisfies.

For as he adds, "Everyone who drinks of this water shall thirst again; but whoever drinks of the water that I shall give him shall never thirst; but the water that I shall give him shall become in him a well of water springing up to eternal life" (Jn. 4:13-14, NASV). Just one drink was necessary. For that one drink became a well of water springing up from within.

So it is true that the garden of one's life may be in disarray. And it is true that the wellsprings of one's life may be impure. But our Creator can accept the garden and restore it. He is the carpenter of Nazareth who constructs a new well in the heart. He offers forgiveness and life as a gift. He promises restoration and virtue as we walk before him.

A Lot to Grasp

Of course, walking before him can mean a good many things. It means living honestly before him, walking in love for him and others in daily trust. It means all this, but let us remember that it also includes trying to practice the principles of romance set forth in our song. What a happy assignment!

Nevertheless, remembering all those principles may not be easy. And understanding what a relationship with Christ is all about may not be simple to grasp at first either. But God has given some helpful illustrations of both. The best illustrations of the principles of romance were probably from our song for lovers. But, as surprising as it may seem at first, these same illustrations also serve as very illuminating illustrations of a relationship with Christ.

Let me explain. The husband's relationship to his wife was meant to be patterned after Christ's relationship to a Christian. That's why the New Testament could tell the husband to love his wife like Christ loved the church. So if a man did love his wife that way, his marriage would be a living illustration of the Lord's relationship to him.

For example, the better a high school quarterback imitated a professional, the more accurately he would model a professional form. And if by chance we knew that a certain high school quarterback were a perfect model, we would know he would perfectly reflect the professional form. Without ever looking at a pro, we would know what a pro would be like by looking at the high school quarterback. By similar reasoning, since we know that in our song we have a model marriage and since we know a marriage should be patterned after Christ's relationship to us, we should expect to find a perfect reflection of Christ's relationship to us.

Now if we can review the principles of romance that emerge from the song and also see how they reflect the Christian's relationship to Christ, two things will be accomplished at once. We will help ourselves remember all the principles of romance and at the same time help ourselves understand a relationship to Christ.

A Very Special Love Song

Let me give a concrete illustration of all this. In the definition of love that the song gave one should expect to find an illustration of Christ's love for the believer. We remember that the king's love was painful, possessive, persevering and priceless. Is Christ's love the same way?

I think we must say yes. Was it not painful both in life and death? Ellen Weldon in *Essays on Love* (IVP) wrote of his life,

> ... *pain is quiet, and love.*
> *And even childbirth pains*
> *Are soundless in themselves*
> *E'en while they tell of love fulfilled.*
> *So came our Lord,*
> *Amid the pain, the ache, the dirt, the hate,*
> *To tell of love.*
> *And as He lived in love, giving it,*
> *Knew the pain as well.*

C. S. Lewis in "Love's As Warm As Tears" wrote of his death,

> *Love's as hard as nails,*
> *Love is nails:*
> *Blunt, thick, hammered through*
> *The medial nerves of One*
> *Who, having made us, knew*
> *The thing He had done,*
> *Seeing (with all that is)*
> *Our cross, and His.*

Even when the great One hung upon the cross he did not turn aside from the pain. When offered the pain-killing drug of "wine mingled with gall," customarily given the sufferer, he refused it, choosing to remain fully conscious as he purchased the grounds for our relationship with himself. How frequently we, on the other hand, drink the drug of bitterness or rationalization to soften the pain accompanying the birth and growth of relationships!

Faced with disappointment with or indifference from someone dear to us, we may choose the anger from bitterness over the acknowledged pain from honestly caring. Or we may choose to rationalize and say, "I don't really care for that person anyway," instead of honestly admitting we do care and hurt, but not hurt so much we will keep from caring. Nevertheless, this reminder of our practice not only humbles us but magnifies the love manifested to us that day on Calvary.

For the one in relationship with Christ there is pain too—the pain of guilt before forgiveness and the pain of trials and adversity. But the guilt awakens us to our need and the trials bring us closer to God; so this pain, also, is the fruitful pain of birth and growth.

Christ's love is possessive too. The apostle Paul spoke of this when he wrote, "For I am convinced that neither death, nor life, nor angels, nor principalities, nor things present, nor things to come, nor powers, nor height, nor depth, nor any other created thing, shall be able to separate us from the love of God, which is in Christ Jesus our Lord" (Rom. 8:38-39, NASV). As Shulamith found her greatest security in the love of her husband, so Paul found his greatest security in the love of Christ. Paul's trust was in the One who gave his life for him. And as Shulamith was like a seal upon the heart and arm of Solomon, so Christians are seals upon the heart and arm of God. For his love is as strong as death; his jealousy is as relentless as Sheol. And although a flood of our problems and sins may test the flame of God, it still burns strongly for us.

His love is also persevering. He will never give us up. Remember the story of the leader whose wife lived like a prostitute? He took her back and gave her a new life in their home. That very story was

God's own illustration of his love for his people. God himself said to them, "I will never desert you, nor will I ever forsake you" (Heb. 13:5, NASV).

Finally, his love is priceless. The Bible says, "For by grace you have been saved through faith; and that not of yourselves, it is a gift of God; not as a result of works, that no one should boast" (Eph. 2:8-9, NASV). The gift of life cannot be purchased with good deeds. In fact, to put a price tag on it and try to pay for it is to insult the giver and try to remove the responsibility love places upon you. You see, if someone gives you a gift of love, your proper response is loving gratitude. But if you can pay for it, then that removes your obligation. God's love at the cross and the gift of eternal life he offers ask for a loving response of faith, a grateful thank you.

But people always want to put a price tag on it. Before becoming Christians they seek to buy their way into God's family by good deeds. But no one's good deeds are good enough to do that. So after becoming Christians they act as if they had purchased the gift on credit. Now they have to work laboriously to pay God back. Of course, it is a priceless gift. They could never pay him back. Just thinking about the gift makes them feel more guilty because they haven't been making enough payments. It's like having a new car with overdue payments. You can't enjoy the car because of the burden it places upon you. Just looking at it is a reminder of your debt.

But God's love is priceless. He'll never demand payment for it. It is a free gift. His love is indeed painful, possessive, persevering and priceless. Isn't it wonderful how the love of our couple illustrates the love of God for us! It does so in a lot of other ways too. In order to help us recall the rest of the principles of romance and to grasp more about our relationship with Christ, let's look at the remaining illustrations in the next chapter.

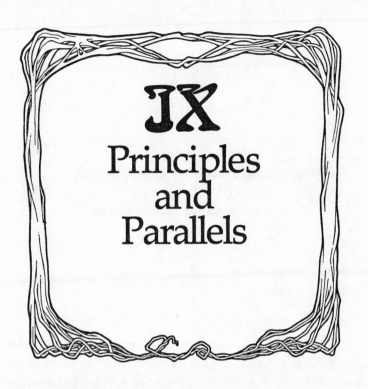

IX
Principles and Parallels

When we see the face of God
we shall know that we have always
known it. He has been . . . within,
all our earthly experiences
of innocent love.
All that was true love in them was, even
on earth, far more His than ours, and
ours only because His.
C. S. Lewis, The Four Loves

NINE

In the Song of Songs it is amazing how the woman's self-image is increasingly heightened by the praise of her lover. She sees herself first as sun-burned and unadorned (1:6) and then as a flower and increasingly the recipient of his affection (2:1). Don't forget how the phrase "My beloved is mine and I am his" eventually became "I am my beloved's and his desire is for me" (2:16; 6:3; 7:11). She is aware that his banner over her is love (2:4). Eventually as she blossoms in the security of marriage, she has the freedom to fully praise him (5:10-16) and to joyfully request they go to the country where she can give her love to him (7:12-14). The Creator designed the woman to be a responder to a man's love.

A Response of Love and Security

One reader of Genesis wrote that "woman was taken from the rib of man—not from his head to be above him, nor from his feet to be walked upon, but from his side to be equal, near his arm to be protected, close to his heart to be loved." She is equal in her privileges before God, yet she is under the loving leadership of her husband. His patient love should bring a response of love and security.

Yet it can also be said that the patient love of Christ brings a response of love and security from the Christian. Over a period of time the woman grew in her security, though she was always the wife of Solomon. Likewise the believer grows in his security in Christ, though he is always a Christian. As Shulamith found her ultimate assurance not in her possession of Solomon but in Solomon's possession and love of her, so the believer finds ultimate assurance not in his possession of Christ but in Christ's possession and love of him. Christ tells us that we are in the Father's hand and nothing can take us out of it (Jn. 10:29). Once we have been born in God's family, we can never be disowned. As parents assume responsibility for a child since they gave birth to him, so God assumes responsibility for us when he gives us spiritual birth (Jas. 1:18). More and more we can trust that his banner over us is love. And as we come to trust more, we will have the confidence to make joyful requests of him in prayer (1 Jn. 3:21-22). The relationship gets better and better.

As a Shepherd and a King He Won His Bride

How significant it is that the king came to the girl he courted also as a shepherd, not anxious to impress her with his kingly possessions but desiring to win her with the inner qualities of his own person. He married her as a king (3:6-11). But he never forgot to identify with her in her country origin. Later in their marriage they still go out to the country in spring recalling where they first courted.

The Lord Jesus Christ also won his bride both as a shepherd and a king. He was always both, yet as Solomon's humble shepherd role was paramount in the beginning of the courtship period though he was recognized as king, so the humility of Christ as shepherd was paramount before his resurrection and exaltation. As Solomon came in marriage as a king to bring her home (3:6-11), so the Lord Jesus will return at the second coming to take us home with him (Jn. 14:1-3; 1 Thess. 4:13-17).

A Reflection of All Relationships

When the king chose his bride, he also chose a lifelong companion, a spiritual sister (5:1), student (8:2) and lover. In some ways she was like a daughter to him. Likewise Solomon was to her friend, companion, brother, father and teacher—all comprising one husband. They found completeness in one another.

Before marriage comes is the time to develop the capacities for all these facets of the relationship. One who can be a close friend, an inquisitive student and a responsible sister or brother may be preparing himself for these facets of a relationship in his marriage. And the more the merrier.

The Lord Jesus is the one in whom we find a complete relationship too. He is our master who leads us yet also our friend who confides in us (Jn. 15:18). He is our servant who cleanses us with forgiveness (Jn. 13:1-10; 1 Jn. 1:9) if only we confess our sins to him. He is also our teacher who instructs us (Mt. 28:18-20). He is our Lord yet also our brother (Rom. 8:29).

Part of the Christian life is cultivating all of these facets of our relationship with Christ. One should never be emphasized at the expense of another. We should not make him just a friend and not honor him with the obedience he deserves as our Lord. Yet he should not be a master who is not also our intimate friend. The more aspects of the relationship we can experience, the more joyful and fulfilling will be our relationship to him.

Certainty and Emotion

Our lovers were certain that each was the perfect one for the other (2:2-3; 6:8-9). They didn't want to date around "just to be sure";

they were in love and they experienced the emotions of love.

The king's bride can become weak from love (2:5); she desires him only (2:3); and they intensely long for one another. In the night she lay awake wanting to be with him (3:1). Only the overflowing life of spring can capture the overflowing life they feel within. Their wedding night is exquisitely portrayed in delicate imagery of passionate restraint (4:1—5:1). As they grow in marriage, their emotional love grows too (7:2-14).

This is an important principle even though it is almost self-evident. Among some people falling in love has about the same status as falling in a ditch. Sometimes these are the modern stoics who believe you should never experience the emotions God gave you. Other times they are the modern cynics who think all emotional love is infatuation based on fantasy.

But there is an infatuation based on reality. And one should not look down on what God has designed. He has evidently designed a true emotional peak to accompany union with one's life partner. True romantic love is neither the invention nor the property of Hollywood but the gift and creation of God.

One's relationship with Christ is also often marked by emotion and certainty. The Christian has the certainty of the Word of God (1 Jn. 5:11-12) and the assurance from the Holy Spirit (Rom. 8:16). Also he is very joyful because every person who becomes a Christian becomes a Christian in spring. The new birth through faith in Christ makes the believer a "new creation" like spring (2 Cor. 5:17). As new life flows through the flowers and trees, so new spiritual life flows through the one who believes in Christ. And such a wonderful miracle brings much joy.

Even under the most dismal circumstances he can be happy because he is with Christ. As a contented wife might be happy wherever she is as long as her husband is there, so the apostle Paul was content wherever he was because he knew that Christ was with him too. In a Roman jail he wrote, "I have learned to be content in whatever circumstance I am. I know how to get along with humble means, and I also know how to live in prosperity; in any and every circumstance I have learned the secret of being filled and going hungry, both of having abundance and suffering need. I can do all things through Him who strengthens me" (Phil. 4:11-13, NASV). Paul's joy and certainty join together when he sincerely says, "For to me, to live is Christ, and to die is gain" (Phil. 1:21, NASV).

Gradual Progression

The courtship of the romance went through two cycles of longing patience and reward, becoming more intense in the process. Then their marriage went from spring to spring with a winter conflict in between. One need only compare their wedding night with a later night of lovemaking to see a progress in openness and freedom.

Impatience may lead a couple to try to take shortcuts to the wedding night or that later night, but God did not design relationships that way. A necessary growth process had to take place before marriage. During this time the two people grew to love and long for one another. Their restraint before marriage prepared them for the beautiful wedding night they experienced together. They also experienced maturing growth in marriage as they patiently worked through problems.

The believer's relationship to Christ is also characterized by gradual progression. When he is born again into God's family, he is a child who must grow through the milk of the Scripture (I Pet. 2:2). To become fully grown will take time and patience as the Spirit of God illuminates him (1 Cor. 2:14—3:2).

To grow physically requires food, exercise and sleep. To grow spiritually requires the food of spiritual teaching, the exercise of practicing it and the restfulness of sleep that comes from faith that God will be working in your life to cause growth. As members of a football team work out together to cause growth and unity of the team, so a believer should "work out" in prayer and fellowship with other Christians to develop maturity and unity with other believers.

Divine Approval

Remember the wedding night of the couple? First he tenderly praised her (4:1-7). Then he called her fearful thoughts to himself (4:8), and they began to make love (4:9-11). Next in the lovely imagery provided by the garden metaphor, they consummated their marriage (4:12—5:1). Finally, however, in the sacred quietness of that moment, the voice of God sealed the night with his approval, "Eat, O loved ones; drink and be drunk, O lovers."

Frequently, because a person's only experience of sex has been associated with guilt, he will come to feel that all sex is wrong. For example, if every time you ate green peas, you were hit over the head with a hammer, you would come to think green peas shouldn't be on the menu. Yet in marriage the sexual expression of love is heartily endorsed by God. That knowledge itself should help change a person's attitude toward sex. God designed it; he endorses it.

Similarly works of gratitude springing from love for Christ are approved by God (Mk. 14:3-9). But in the same way that sex without love or apart from marriage is empty and wrong, so good works without love for Christ or a relationship with him are cold and unprofitable. They will not help an unbeliever gain new birth, and they will not enrich the life of a believer unless they come from love (Rev. 2:1-5). If a wife really loves her husband, she will derive much joy from doing things for him. But if her love has grown cold, these same things will be a burden to her. Likewise, when a believer loves Christ, he will derive much joy from serving him. But if his love has grown cold toward Christ, the same things will become a burden to him.

Reconciliation in Conflict

When his wife becomes more concerned about her own comfort and appearance than about loving her husband, the first problem arose in their marriage (5:1-8). Her neglect of him led to their temporary separation from each other. And while they were separated, other things went wrong too. Remember, the watchmen of the city just compounded her problem in pounding her! Yet the misery of separation reawakened her to an appreciation of her husband (5:10-16). When she went to see him in the garden, she was met with the praises of forgiveness (6:1-9). Before she knew it they were together again, getting along better than ever before (6:10-13). Then she was readily recognized as Shulamith, Solomon's feminine counterpart.

This whole sequence of events is frequently paralleled in one's relationship to Christ. The initial excitement of the new relationship carries one along for a while, but then the day-to-day living with him may lull the new Christian into ingratitude and more concern for himself than for Christ. This eventually will lead to an actual event that causes separation, just as the wife's ingratitude and listless response to her husband led to their separation. The Christian is then aware of the loss of the closeness of his relationship to Christ. And as if that is not enough, it seems that other problems soon follow.

Sometimes this represents divine discipline meant to awaken us to the seriousness of our predicament. But thankfully this often leads to renewed appreciation of the great One whom we now know and to a desire to experience a close relationship again with him.

However, just as the woman even in the midst of separation could affirm that "I am my beloved's and my beloved is mine," so the Christian can still rest assured that he belongs to Christ even when he fails to live for Christ like he should. One who is married doesn't always experience the same closeness in that marriage. But when the believer goes to Christ in confession of sin he is always met by forgiveness. As the husband communicated to his wife that she was still the woman he married, so Christ tells us that we are still as cleansed as the day we were born into his family. When we take our guilty eyes off ourselves, we look to him and see how he views us. Then looking back at ourselves through his eyes of forgiveness, we see ourselves cleansed and close to him again.

Often it is only after conflict that we are experientially made more like Christ. People can tell we are really Christians after a certain degree of suffering has made us more like our master who suffered. As Shulamith was recognized as Solomon's counterpart only after her conflict and reconciliation with him, so the believer is often better recognized as a follower of Christ after conflict and reconciliation with him.

Remember Shulamith experienced two kinds of suffering—deserved and undeserved. Deservedly she suffered pain from ingratitude, but perhaps undeservedly she suffered pain from the watchmen of the city. Both kinds of pain can help a person to be more Christ-like.

The first may help him reaffirm his determination to be closer to Christ so that separation might not occur again. But when we suffer undeservedly, it may be far better. If we bear up under it without complaining, we are being like Christ because although he never deserved to suffer, he bore up under it without complaint. In doing so he bore the penalty for sin and gave us life. So although both kinds of suffering can bring us closer to Christ, undeserved suffering may be more profitable to experience.

Both Human Responsibility and Divine Providence

In the song for lovers the family of the bride had helped prepare her for marriage through both discipline and encouragement (8:8-9). Yet she herself assumed responsibility for her preparation for marriage, too, in determining to keep herself for her husband (8:10). Then in the providential arrangement of God she met her husband in very unpromising circumstances (1:6; 8:10-11).

Similarly God may use a number of means to bring a person to Christ. Family or friends who cared enough to pray for him and to share with him the message of Christ may be part of the means. And as Shulamith had to respond to Solomon if she wished marriage, so the person must respond by faith in Christ to gain eternal life. The person is a responsible means too. But ultimately God providentially brings every person to Christ who comes, and he enables the person to believe. So in the final analysis the Scripture can give all the glory to God for the new life he gives to every Christian (Eph. 1:4-6). The one who thinks often of this cannot help but be one who always is thankful.

X

Shadow
and
Reality

Where there is love
there is trinity:
a lover,
a beloved
and a spirit of love.
Augustine

TEN

When the nature of God is mentioned and the concept of the Trinity is introduced, the fog seems to set in for most people. God the Father, God the Son and God the Holy Spirit—three Persons yet one God. How can this be the case? How can we understand it?

Well, the Scriptures do teach it. There's no doubt of that. And God would not have taught it if he thought that everyone would be totally confused by it. A lot of theologians have devised what they thought were good illustrations of it. They talk about steam, water and ice as all being water. Or they point to the three separate sides of the triangle as still being one triangle.

But these illustrations aren't really accurate. In the first one, the same water is the steam, water and ice. Yet the Scripture is not teaching simply that one person is existing in three forms. The second illustration leads one to believe that it takes all three persons to equal one God; yet the Scripture teaches that each Person is fully God.

It's interesting that God never gave illustrations of the Trinity.

But he comes very close to it a couple of times. Would you believe that the illustration he gives of himself is the marriage relationship? In Genesis he says, "Let us make man in our image." (Notice the "us" assumes more than one person in the one God.) The Scripture adds, "God created man in His own image, in the image of God He created him; male and female created He them." Man plus woman equals Man. One plus one equals one, for the two "shall become one" (Gen. 2:24, NASV).

Then the New Testament says, "Christ is the head of every man, and the man is the head of a woman, and God is the head of Christ" (1 Cor. 11:3, NASV). God is the "head" of Christ as man is the "head" of woman. In some way the Father relates to the Son as the husband relates to his wife. Perhaps the way is that in both cases there is equality but leadership. The Father is equal to the Son but the Father initiates, and the Son delights to do his will. Likewise the husband initiates, and the wife delights to respond. So the Trinity is reflected somewhat in the marriage relationship. The Trinity is the reality of which marriage is but a shadow.

But what about the Holy Spirit? Admittedly, the illustration is not as clear at this point. But perhaps the words of a truly great theologian named Augustine can help here. He said, "Where there is love there is trinity: a lover, a beloved and a spirit of love." The spirit of love between a couple may be an illustration of the Spirit.

"So what," you may say. "Why is this important?" I think it is important because it gives us a brief glimpse into the very nature of God himself, and there is no higher kind of knowledge than the knowledge of him. For just a moment the curtain is lifted and we can faintly glimpse the love relationship that existed before the world began. Think of it—before the stars and planets of the universe were ever set in the skies, the Father eternally loved the Son and the Son delighted to respond to the Father, and the Holy Spirit related with them in an eternal Trinity of love. It is a wonderful truth. No wonder Christ mentions it when He prays to His Father: "For you loved me before the foundation of the world" (Jn. 17:24).

Some philosophers have wondered how there could be such a thing as a loving God before there were people to love. "God needs us in order that he might have someone to love," they want to reply. Or "The world must always have been here so God would have someone to love." Yet they do not recognize that the great Triune God of Scripture is sufficient in his tri-personal self to love without the world. God doesn't need us that he might love someone, but we desperately need him that he might love us!

But the Trinity is more than an answer to a philosopher's problem. It is a great comfort and assurance to his children. Psychologists tell us that the best thing a husband can do for his child is to love their mother. The children will then know that the foundation of their home is a love independent of them.

In the same way when we recognize that God is truly Love himself in that the Father eternally loves the Son in the fellowship of the Spirit—when we recognize this, we realize that the foundation of our home in him is a love independent of us. He does not wring his hands and worry with the Son when we step out of line. In overflowing love he continually brings his children to an experience of the love he has experienced eternally.

AN INTERPRETIVE PARAPHRASE OF THE SONG OF SOLOMON

Many songwriters have discovered a wealth of popular songs in the melodies of the past. Bach has been adapted. Old English folk tunes have too. The melody of Scarborough Fair, for example, goes back to merry old England. But someone had to find it and adapt it to the modern ear. Thanks to Simon and Garfunkel and others we can newly appreciate the older melodies. For us they live again.

In order to make the melody of the old Song of Songs live again for us, I have tried to interpret and explain it in a way meaningful to us who live in the twentieth century. Now let me summarize that interpretation by adapting the entire song to the modern ear. Listen again to the song for lovers in modern language.

The Most Beautiful Love Song Ever Written

Shulamith's First Days in the Palace (1:2-11)

The King's fiancée, Shulamith, in soliloquy

How I wish he would shower me with kisses for his exquisite kisses are more desirable than the finest wine. The gentle fragrance of your cologne brings the enchantment of springtime. Yes it is the rich fragrance of your heart that awakens my love and respect. Yes, it is your character that brings you admiration from every girl of the court. How I long for you to come take me with you to run and laugh through the countryside of this kingdom. (You see, the King had brought me to the kingdom's palace.)

Women of the court to the King

We will always be very thankful and happy because of you, O King. For we love to speak of the inspiring beauty of your love.

Shulamith in soliloquy

They rightly love a person like you, my King.

Shulamith to women of the court

I realize that I do not display the fair and delicate skin of one raised in the comfort of a palace. I am darkened from the sun—indeed, as dark as the tents of the humble desert nomads I used to work beside. But now I might say that I am also as dark as the luxurious drapery of the King's palace. Nevertheless, what loveliness I do have is not so weak that the gaze of the sun should make it bow its head in shame. And if the glare of the sun could not shame me, please know that neither will the glare of your contempt. I could not help it that my stepbrothers were angry with me and demanded that I work in the vineyard they had leased from the King. It was impossible for me to care for it and for the vineyard of my own appearance.

Shulamith to King

Please tell me, you whom I love so deeply, where you take your royal flock for its afternoon rest. I don't want to search randomly for you, wandering about like a woman of the streets.

Women of the court to Shulamith

If you do not know, O fairest among women, why not simply go ahead and follow the trail of the flocks, and then pasture your flock beside the shepherds' huts?

King to Shulamith

Your presence captivates attention as thoroughly as a single mare among a hundred stallions. And how perfectly your lovely jewelry and necklace adorn your lovely face.

Women of the court to Shulamith

We shall make even more elegant necklaces of gold and silver to adorn her face.

In a Palace Room (1:12-14)

Shulamith in soliloquy

While my King was dining at his table, my perfume refreshed me with its soothing fragrance. For my King is the fragrance and my thoughts of him are like a sachet of perfume hung around my neck, over my heart, continually refreshing me. How dear he is to me, as dear as the delicate henna blossoms in the oasis of En-Gedi. What joy I have found in that oasis!

In the Countryside (1:15—2:7)

King to Shulamith

You are so beautiful, my love. You are so beautiful. Your soft eyes are as gentle as doves.

Shulamith to King

And you are handsome, my love, and so enjoyable. It's so wonderful to walk through our home of nature together. Here the cool grass is a soft couch to lie upon, to catch our breath and to gaze at the beams and rafters of our house—the towering cedars and cypresses all around. Lying here I feel like a rose from the valley of Sharon, the loveliest flower in the valley.

King to Shulamith

Only the loveliest flower in the valley? No, my love. To me you are like a flower among thorns compared with any other woman in the world.

Shulamith to King

And you, my precious King, are like a fruitful apple tree among the barren trees of the forest compared with all the men in the world.

Shulamith in soliloquy

No longer do I labor in the heat of the sun. I find cool rest in the shade of this apple tree. Nourishment from its magical fruit brings me the radiant health only love brings. And he loves me so much. Even when he brings me to the great royal banquets attended by the most influential people in this kingdom and beyond, he is never so concerned for them that his love and his care for me is not as plain as a royal banner lifted high above my head.

How dear he is to me! My delightful peace in his love makes me so weak from joy that I must rest in his arms for strength. Yet such loving comfort makes me more joyful and weaker still. How I wish he could lay me down beside him and embrace me! But how important it is I promise, with the gentle gazelles and deer of the countryside as my witnesses, not to attempt to awaken love until love is pleased to awaken itself.

On the Way to the Countryside (2:8-17)

Shulamith in soliloquy

I hear my beloved. Look! He is coming to visit. And he is as dashing as a young stag leaping upon the mountains, springing upon the hills. There he is, standing at the door, trying to peer through the window and peep through the lattice. At last he speaks.

King to Shulamith

Come, my darling, my fair one, come with me. For look, the winter has passed. The rain is over and gone. The blossoms have appeared in the land. The time of singing has come, and the voice of the turtledove has been heard in the land. The fig tree has ripened its figs, and the vines in blossom have given forth fragrance. Let us go, my darling, my lovely one; come along with me. O my precious, gentle dove. You have been like a dove in the clefts of the mountain rocks, in the hidden places along the mountain trails. Now come out from the hidden place and let me see you. Let me hear the coo of your voice. For your voice is sweet and you are as gracefully beautiful as a dove in flight silhouetted against a soft blue sky. My love, what we have together is a valuable treasure; it is like a garden of the loveliest flowers in the world. Let us promise each other to catch any foxes that could spoil our garden when now at long last it blossoms for us.

Shulamith in soliloquy

My beloved belongs to me and I belong to him—this tender King who grazes his flock among the lilies.

Shulamith to the King

How I long for the time when all through the night, until the day takes its first breath and the morning shadows flee from the sun, that you, my beloved King, might be a gazelle upon the hills of my breasts.

Shulamith Waits for Her Fiancé (3:1-5)

Shulamith in soliloquy

How I miss the one I love so deeply. I could not wait to see him. I thought to myself, "I must get up and find him. I will get up now and look around the streets and squares of the city for him. Surely I'll be able to find this one I love so much." But I could not find him. When the night watchmen of the city found me, I immediately asked them if they had seen this one I loved so deeply. But they had not. Yet no sooner did I pass from them than I found my beloved. I held on and on and would not let him go until I could bring him to my home. I still held on until my fearful anxieties left me and I felt peaceful once again. How hard it is to be patient! You women of the court, we must promise ourselves, by the gazelles and deer of the field, not to awaken love until love is pleased to awaken itself.

The Wedding Day (3:6-11)

Poet

What can this be coming from the outskirts of the city like columns of smoke, perfumed clouds of myrrh and frankincense, clouds of the scented powders of the merchant? Look! It is the royal procession with Solomon carried upon his lavish couch by his strongest servants. And take a look at all those soldiers around it! That is the imperial guard, the sixty mightiest warriors in the entire kingdom. Each one is an expert with his weapon and valiant in battle. Yet now each one has a sword at his side only for the protection of the King and his bride. Look at the luxurious couch Solomon is carried on. He has had it made especially for this day. He made its frame from the best timber of Lebanon. Its posts are made of silver, its back of gold, and its seat of royal purple cloth. And do you see its delicate craftsmanship! It reflects the skill of the women of the court who gave their best work out of love for the King and his bride. Let us all go out and look upon King Solomon wearing his elegant wedding crown. Let us go out and see him on the most joyful day of his life.

The Wedding Night (4:1—5:1)

King to Shulamith

You are so beautiful, my love, you are so beautiful. Your soft eyes are as gentle as doves from behind your wedding veil. Your hair is as captivating as the flowing movement of a flock descending a mountain at sunset. Your full and lovely smile is as cheerful and sparkling as pairs of young lambs scurrying up from a washing. And only a thread of scarlet could have outlined your lips so perfectly. Your cheeks flush with the redness of the pomegranate's hue. Yet you walk with dignity and stand with the strength of a fortress. Your necklace sparkles like the shields upon the fortress tower. But your breasts are as soft and gentle as fawns grazing among lilies. And now at last, all through the night—until the day takes its first breath and the morning shadows flee from the sun—I will be a gazelle upon the hills of your perfumed breasts. You are completely and perfectly beautiful, my love, and flawless in every way. Now bring your thoughts completely to me, my love. Leave your fears in the far away mountains and rest in the security of my arms.

You excite me, my darling bride; you excite me with but a

glance of your eyes, with but a strand of your necklace. How wonderful are your caresses, my beloved bride. Your love is more sweetly intoxicating than the finest wine. And the fragrance of your perfume is better than the finest spices. The richness of honey and milk is under your tongue, my love. And the fragrance of your garments is like the fragrance of the forests of Lebanon.

You are a beautiful garden fashioned only for me, my darling bride. Yes, like a garden kept only for me. Or like a fresh fountain sealed just for me. Your garden is overflowing with beautiful and delicate flowers of every scent and color. It is a paradise of pomegranates with luscious fruit, with henna blossoms and nard, nard and saffron, calamus and cinnamon with trees of frankincense, myrrh and aloes with all the choicest of spices. And you are pure as fresh water, yet more than a mere fountain. You are a spring for many gardens—a well of life-giving water. No, even more, you are like the fresh streams flowing from Lebanon which give life to the entire countryside.

Shulamith to King

Awake, O north wind, and come, wind of the south. Let your breezes blow upon my garden and carry its fragrant spices to my beloved. May he follow the enchanting spices to my garden and come in to enjoy its luscious fruit.

King to Shulamith

I have rejoiced in the richness of your garden, my darling bride. I have been intoxicated by the fragrance of your myrrh and perfume. I have tasted the sweetness of your love like honey. I have enjoyed the sweetness of your love like an exquisite wine and the refreshment of your love like the coolness of milk.

Poet to couple

Rejoice in your lovemaking as you would rejoice at a great feast, O lovers. Eat and drink from this feast to the fullest. Drink, drink and be drunk with one another's love.

A Problem Arises (5:2—6:3)

Shulamith in soliloquy

I was half asleep when I heard the sound of my beloved husband knocking gently upon the door of our palace chamber. He whispered softly, "I'm back from the countryside, my love, my darling, my perfect wife." My only answer was a mumbled, "I've already gone to sleep, my dear." After all, I had already prepared for bed. I had washed my face and put on my old nightgown.

But then my beloved gently opened the door and I realized I really wanted to see him. I had hesitated too long though. By the time I arose to open the door, he had already walked away, leaving only a gift of my favorite perfume as a reminder of his love for me. Deep within my heart I was reawakened to my love for him. It was just that the fatigue and distractions of the day had brought my hesitating response. I decided to try to find him. I threw on my clothes, went outside the palace and began to call out to him.

But things went from bad to worse. The night watchmen of the city mistook me for a secretive criminal sneaking about in the night. They arrested me in their customarily rough style, then jerking my shawl from my head they saw the face of their newly found suspect—a "great" police force we have!

O, you women of the court, if you see my beloved King, please tell him that I deeply love him, that I am lovesick for him.

Women of the court to Shulamith

What makes your husband better than any other, O fairest of women? What makes him so great that you request this so fervently of us?

Shulamith to women of the court

My beloved husband is strikingly handsome, the first to be noticed among ten thousand men. When I look at him, I see a face with a tan more richly golden than gold itself. His hair is as black as a raven's feathers and as lovely as palm leaves atop the stately palm tree. When I look into his eyes, they are as gentle as doves peacefully resting by streams of water. They are as pure and clear as health can make them.

When he places his cheek next to mine, it is as fragrant as a garden of perfumed flowers. His soft lips are as sweet and scented as lilies dripping with nectar. And how tender are his fingers like golden velvet when he touches me! He is a picture of strength and vitality. His stomach is as firm as a plate of ivory rippling with sapphires. And his legs are as strong and elegant as alabaster pillars set upon pedestals of fine gold. His appearance is like majestic Mt. Lebanon, prominent with its towering cedars.

But beyond all this, the words of his heart are full of charm and delight. He is completely wonderful in every way. This is the one I love so deeply, and this is the one who is my closest friend, O women of the palace court.

Women of the court to Shulamith

Where has your beloved gone, then, O fairest among women? Where has he gone? We will help you find him.

Shulamith to women of the court

Oh, I know him well enough to know where he has gone. He likes to contemplate as he walks through the garden and cares for his special little flock among the lilies. I know him, for I belong to him and he belongs to me—this gentle shepherd who pastures his flock among the lilies.

The Problem Resolved (6:4-13)

King to Shulamith

My darling, did you know that you are as lovely as the city of

Tirzah glittering on the horizon of night? No, more than that you are as lovely as the fair city of Jerusalem. Your beauty is as breathtaking as scores of marching warriors. (No, do not look at me like that now, my love; I have more to tell you.)

Do you remember what I said on our wedding night? It is still just as true. Your hair is as captivating as the flowing movement of a flock descending a mountain at sunset. Your lovely smile is as cheerful and sparkling as pairs of young lambs scurrying up from a washing. And your cheeks still flush with the redness of the pomegranate's hue.

King in soliloquy

The palace is full of its aristocratic ladies and dazzling mistresses belonging to the noblemen of the court. But my lovely wife, my dove, my flawless one, is unique among them all. And these ladies and mistresses realize it too. They too must praise her. As we approached them in my chariot, they eventually perceived that we were together again.

Women of the court to one another

Who is that on the horizon like the dawn, now fair as the moon but now plain and bright as the sun and as majestic as scores of marching warriors?

Shulamith in the chariot in soliloquy

I went down to the garden where I knew my King would be. I wanted to see if the fresh flowers and fruits of spring had come. I wanted to see if our reunion might bring a new season of spring love for my husband and me. Before I knew what happened, we were together again and riding past the palace court in his chariot. I can still hear them calling out, "Return, return O Shulamith; return that we may gaze at the beloved wife of the King."

King to Shulamith

How they love to look upon the incomparable grace and beauty of a queen.

In the Royal Bedroom (7:1-10)

King to Shulamith

How delicate are your feet in sandals, my royal prince's daughter! The curves of your hips are as smooth and graceful as the curves of elegant jewelry, perfectly fashioned by the skillful hands of a master artist. As delectable as a feast of wine and bread is your stomach—your navel is like the goblet of wine, and your stomach is the soft warm bread. Your breasts are as soft and gentle as fawns grazing among lilies, twins of a gazelle, and your neck is smooth as ivory to the touch. Your eyes are as peaceful as the pools of water in the valley of Heshbon, near the gate of the populous city.

Yet how strong you walk in wisdom and discretion. You are, indeed, as majestically beautiful as Mt. Carmel. Your long flowing hair is as cool and soft as silken threads draped round my neck, yet strong enough to bind me as your captive forever. How lovely and delightful you are, my dear, and how especially delightful is your love! You are as graceful and splendrous as a palm tree silhouetted against the sky. Yes, a palm tree—and your breasts are its luscious fruit.

I think I shall climb my precious palm tree and take its tender fruit gently into my hand. O my precious one, let your breasts be like the tender fruit to my taste, and now let me kiss you and breathe your fragrant breath. Let me kiss you and taste a sweetness better than wine.

Shulamith to King

And savor every drop, my lover, and let its sweetness linger long upon your lips, and let every drop of this wine bring a peaceful sleep.

Shulamith in soliloquy

I belong to my beloved husband and he loves me from the depths of his soul.

In the Countryside (7:11—8:14)

Shulamith to King

Spring's magic flowers have perfumed the pastel countryside
and enchanted the hearts of all lovers. Come, my precious lover;
every delicious fruit of spring is ours for the taking. Let us return
to our springtime cottage of towering cedars and cypresses
where the plush green grass is its endless carpet and the orchards
are its shelves for every luscious fruit. I have prepared a basketful
for you, my love, to give you in a sumptuous banquet of love
beneath the sky.

I wish we could pretend you were my brother, my real little
brother. I could take you outside to play, and playfully kiss you
whenever I wished. But then I could also take your hand and
bring you inside and you could teach me and share with me your
deep understanding of life. Then how I wish you would lay me
down beside you and love me.

Shulamith to women of the court

I encourage you not to try to awaken love until love is pleased to
awaken itself. How wonderful it is when it blossoms in the
proper season.

Shulamith to King

Do you remember where our love began? Under the legendary
sweetheart tree, of course, where every love begins and grows
and then brings forth a newborn child, yet not without the pain
of birth. Neither did our love begin without the pain, the fruitful
pain of birth. O, my darling lover, make me your most precious
possession held securely in your arms, held close to your heart.
True love is as strong and irreversible as the onward march of
death. True love never ceases to care, and it would no more give
up the beloved than the grave would give up the dead.

The fires of true love can never be quenched because the
source of its flame is God himself. Even were a river of rushing

water to pass over it, the flame would yet shine forth. Of all the gifts in the world, this priceless love is the most precious and possessed only by those to whom it is freely given. For no man could purchase it with money, even the richest man in the world.

King to Shulamith

Do you remember how it was given to us?

Shulamith to King

My love, I truly believe I was being prepared for it long before I even dreamed of romance. I remember hearing my brothers talking one evening. It was shortly after my father died, and they were concerned to raise me properly, to prepare me for the distant day of marriage. They were like a roomful of fathers debating about what to do with their only daughter. They finally resolved simply to punish and restrict me if I were promiscuous but to reward and encourage me if I were chaste. How thankful I am that I made it easy for them. I could see even when I was very young that I wanted to keep myself for the one dearest man in my life.

And then you came. And everything I ever wanted I found in you. There I was, working daily in the vineyard my brothers had leased from you. And you "happened" to pass by and see me. That's how our love began.

I remember when I worked in that vineyard that a thousand dollars went to you and two hundred dollars for the ones taking care of its fruit for you. Now I am your vineyard, my lover, and I gladly give the entire thousand dollars of my worth to you; I give myself completely, withholding nothing of my trust, my thoughts, my care, my love. But my dear King, let us not forget that two hundred dollars belongs to the ones who took care of the fruit of my vineyard for you. How thankful we must be to my family who helped prepare me for you.

King to Shulamith
My darling, whose home is the fragrant garden, everyone listens for the sound of your voice, but let me alone hear it now.

Shulamith to King
Hurry, then, my beloved. And again be like a gazelle or young stag on the hills of my perfumed breasts.

A MODERN ENGLISH
TRANSLATION
OF THE
SONG OF SOLOMON

Preceding each section of the poem are the designations of speaker and addressee. These designations are not part of the original text. Rather they are inferred from the verses themselves—either from the titles of address or from the second person pronoun which, unlike in English, distinguishes between the masculine and the feminine. Frequently both of these indicators are present to allow identification. When they are lacking, however, the identification of either speaker or addressee is occasionally a bit uncertain. In these few instances the uncertainty is disclosed by putting the speaker or addressee in parentheses, by adding a footnote or by including both.

There are also words in parentheses within the translation itself. These are not strictly a part of the original text, but they are inserted either for smoothness, or perhaps simply because of an obvious ellipsis in the original. Where there is some question on the propriety of these insertions, explanation by footnote accompanies it. Where necessity is self-evident, no footnote is given. Other difficult translation problems have also been appropriately footnoted.

It might also be observed that this translation approximates the New American Standard Version more closely than any other translation. But it also differs from it in many crucial passages. The entire translation was from the Massoretic Text with the use of common lexicographical and grammatical tools. However, occasionally a translation was governed by an uncommon specialized source (e.g. Nahum B. Waldman, "A Note on Canticles 4.9 and 6.5," Journal of Biblical Literature, *89 [June, 1970], pp. 216-217).*

Finally, the bride's affectionate title for her lover, dôdh, was consistently rendered "beloved." One of the king's affectionate titles for his bride, ra'yah, was consistently rendered "darling."

1:1   The Song of Songs which is Solomon's.

Bride (in soliloquy)

2   Oh, that he would kiss me with the kisses of his mouth,
        for better than wine is your affection.

3   For fragrance your perfumes are pleasing,
        and perfume poured forth is your name.
    Therefore, the maidens love you.

4   Draw me after you! Let us run together!
    The king has brought me to his chambers.

Daughters of Jerusalem to King

    We will rejoice and be glad in you.
    We will extol your love (better)[1] than wine.

Bride[2] (in soliloquy)[3]

    Rightly do they love you.

---

[1]The ellipses of *tôbhîm* from 1:2 is assumed.

[2]The third person plural verb, "they love," indicates an observer of those speaking in 4b, "we will rejoice... extol."

[3]The soliloquy is assumed to be an extension of the same kind of speech given in 1:2-4; though it is possible she directly addresses the king here.

to Daughters of Jerusalem

5   Dark am I but lovely, O daughters of Jerusalem,
        like the tents of Kedar,
        like the curtains of Solomon.

6   Do not stare at me for I am dark;
        the sun has scorched me.
    My mother's sons were angry with me.
    They appointed me caretaker of the vineyards,
        but of my own vineyard—which belongs to me—
    I have not taken care.

(in soliloquy)[4]

7   Tell me, O you whom my soul loves,
        where you pasture your flock,
        where you rest them at noon,
        lest I become as a veiled woman by the flocks
        of your companions.

Daughters of Jerusalem to Bride

8   If you do not know, O most beautiful among women,
        go forth on the trail of the flock
        and pasture your young goats by the tents
        of the shepherds.

King to Bride

9   To a mare among the chariots of Pharaoh
        I liken you my darling.

10   Lovely are your cheeks with ornaments
        and your neck with strings of beads.

Daughters of Jerusalem to Bride

11   Chains of gold will we make for you
        with points of silver.

---

[4]This is assumed to be a soliloquy because the answer to her question comes not from the king but from the daughters of Jerusalem. Once again, however, it is possible she directly addresses him.

Bride in soliloquy

12   While the king was at his table,
        my nard gave its fragrance.

13   A pouch of myrrh is my beloved to me
        which lies all night between my breasts.

14   My beloved is to me a cluster of henna blossoms
        in the vineyards of En-Gedi.

King to Bride

15   Behold, you are beautiful my darling; behold you
        are beautiful;
        Your eyes are doves.

Bride to King

16   Behold, you are handsome my beloved; indeed you are
        pleasant.
        And our couch is verdant.[5]

17   The beams of our houses are cedars;
        our rafters, cypresses.

2:1   I am a rose of Sharon,
        a lily of the valley.

King to Bride

2   As a lily among thorns,
        thus is my darling among the young women.

Bride (to King)

3   As an apple tree among the trees of the forest,
        so is my beloved among the young men.
        In his shade I took great delight and sat down,
        and his fruit was sweet to my taste.

---

[5]The word *ra'ananah* rendered "verdant," is an agricultural term for the state of being healthy or in season, as a tree in blossom or grass that is green. The implication is that they rest upon the grass which serves as a couch. The image is carried further in 1:17 with the plural "houses" (for all outdoors is their home) comprised of natural trees.

A SONG FOR LOVERS

(in soliloquy)

4   He has brought me to the banquet hall,
and his banner over me is love.

(to King)

5   Sustain me with raisin cakes and refresh me with apples
for I am faint with love.

(in soliloquy)

6   Oh that his left hand were under my head and his right
hand embraced me.[6]

to Daughters of Jerusalem

7   I adjure you, O daughters of Jerusalem,
by the gazelles or the hinds of the field
not to arouse, not to awaken love until it pleases.[7]

(in soliloquy)

8   The sound of my beloved,
Behold, he is coming,
leaping over the mountains, bounding over the hills.

9   My beloved is like a gazelle or a young stag.
Look, he is standing behind our wall,
gazing through the windows,

---

[6]Either a jussive or progressive imperfect sense may be given *tehabbeqenî* morphologically; however, the jussive is believed to be more appropriate to this context (so also NASB, RSV, Berkeley Version).

[7]The occasional translation rendered by others ("Do not arouse nor awaken *my* love until *she* pleases") is quite unlikely. Admittedly the verb "pleases," like all Hebrew verbs of this form, may contain either a feminine or a neuter subject. The feminine is unlikely, however, for two reasons. First, it would assume that the man is speaking. Yet here, as well as in the repetitions of this refrain in 3:7 and 8:4, the bride is clearly the one speaking beforehand. Second, '*ahabhah* is not a title used by the king for his bride. Normally it is the mental love from which proceeds the caresses of love, the *dôdhîm*. The former is abstract, the latter concrete. In other words, the abstract '*ahabhah* would not likely refer to a concrete person as in "my love." Hence the "my," which is not in the original Hebrew and wrongly inferred, should be omitted. The translation should therefore be "Do not arouse nor awaken love until it pleases." An extended discussion of this may be found in S. Craig Glickman, *The Unity of the Song of Solomon*, Thesis, Dallas Theological Seminary, 1974, pp. 99-102.

peering through the lattice.

10 My beloved responded and said to me,
"Arise my darling, my fair one, and come.

11 For behold, the winter has passed.
The rain is over and gone.

12 The blossoms have appeared in the land.
The time of singing has come,
and the cooing of the turtledove is heard in our land.

13 The fig tree forms its figs,
and the vines in blossom give forth fragrance.
Arise, my darling, my beautiful one, and come along.

14 O my dove, in the clefts of the rocks,
in the hidden places of the steep pathway,
Let me see your form; let me hear your voice.
For your voice is sweet, and your form is lovely.

15 Let us catch the foxes—the little foxes who ruin vineyards,
for our vineyards are in blossom."

16 My beloved is mine and I am his—he who pastures his flock
among the lilies.

17 Until the day breathes and the shadows flee,
turn, my beloved, and be like a gazelle or a
young stag on the mountains of separation.[8]

(in soliloquy)

3:1 Upon my bed in the night I sought him whom my soul loves.
I sought him but did not find him.

2 I will arise now and go about in the city,
in the streets and in the squares.
I will seek him whom my soul
loves.
I sought him but did not find him.

---

[8]The word rendered "of separation" might also be "of cleavage" or "of Bether";
if "separation" or "cleavage," it likely refers to her breasts.

3   The watchmen who go about in the city found me.
     (I said), "Have you seen him
       whom my soul loves?"
4   Scarcely had I passed from them when I found him
       whom my soul loves.
     I held on to him and would not let him go
       until I brought him to the house of my mother,
       to the room of the one who conceived me.

to the Daughters of Jerusalem
5   I adjure you, O daughters of Jerusalem,
       by the gazelles or the hinds of the field
       not to arouse, not to awaken love until it pleases.

Poet
6   What is this coming from the wilderness
       like columns of smoke,
       from the burning of myrrh and frankincense
       made from all the scented powders of the merchant?
7   Behold! It is the couch of Solomon.
     Sixty mighty men around it from the mighty men of Israel.
8   All of them wielders of the sword, trained for battle;
     Each, his sword at his side
       (for protection) from the terrors of the night.
9   A palanquin King Solomon made for himself
       from the timber of Lebanon.
10   He made its posts of silver, its back of gold,
       its seat of purple cloth, its interior inlaid
       with expressions of love from the daughters of Jerusalem.
11   Go forth, O daughters of Zion, and look upon King
       Solomon with the crown with which his mother has
       crowned him on the day of his wedding
       and on the day of the gladness of his heart.

King to Bride

4:1 Behold, you are beautiful, my darling; behold,
   you are beautiful.
   Your eyes are doves from behind your veil.
   Your hair is like a flock of goats which descend
   from Mount Gilead.

2 Your teeth are like a flock of newly shorn sheep
   which have come up from the washing,
   all of which are paired,
      and not one of them is alone.

3 Like a scarlet thread are your lips,
   and your mouth is lovely.
   Your temples are like a slice of a pomegranate
   behind your veil.

4 Like the tower of David is your neck, built for warfare[9]—
   a thousand shields hang upon it,
   all the shields of the mighty men.

5 Your two breasts are like two fawns, twins of a gazelle,
   which feed among the lilies.

6 Until the day breathes and the shadows flee,
   I will go my way to the mountain of myrrh
   and hill of frankincense.

7 You are altogether fair, my love, and there is
   no blemish in you.

8 With me from Lebanon, O bride, with me from Lebanon
   come.
   Journey from the peak of Amana,
      from the peak of Senir and Hermon,
         from the dens of lions and the mountains of leopards.

9 You have made my heart beat fast, my sister, my bride.

---

[9]The word *lethalpîyôth*, rendered "for warfare," is uncertain in meaning.

You have made my heart beat fast
with one glance of your eyes,
with one jewel of your necklace.

10 How beautiful are your caresses, my sister, my bride.
How much better are your caresses than wine
and the fragrance of your perfumes
than any spice.

11 Your lips, (my) bride, drip honey;
Honey and milk are under your tongue,
and the fragrance of your garments is like
the fragrance of Lebanon.

12 A garden locked is my sister, (my) bride.
A spring locked, a fountain sealed.

13 Your shoots are a paradise of pomegranates
with excellent fruit,
henna blossoms with nard plants,

14 nard and saffron, calamus and cinnamon,
with all trees of frankincense,
myrrh and aloes with all the choicest of spices,

15 a garden fountain, a well of living water
and streams flowing from Lebanon.

Bride to King
16 Awake, O north wind.
And come, wind of the south.
Blow upon my garden and let its spices flow forth.
May my beloved come to his garden and eat
its excellent fruit.

King to Bride
5:1 I have come into my garden, my sister, my bride.
I have gathered my myrrh with my balsam.
I have eaten my honeycomb with my honey.
I have drunk my wine with my milk.

Poet to Bride and King
  Eat, O loved ones;
  Drink and be drunk, O lovers.[10]
Bride to Daughters of Jerusalem
2 I was asleep but my heart was awake.

  The sound of my beloved knocking,
  "Open to me my sister, my darling, my dove, my perfect
   one, for my hair is filled with dew; my hair, with damp
   of the night."
3 I had put off my tunic; must I put it on again?

  I had washed my feet; must I soil them again?
4 My beloved withdrew his hand from the door,
   and my feelings were aroused for him.
5 I arose to open to my beloved
   and my hand dripped with myrrh
   and my fingers with flowing myrrh upon the handles
   of the bolt.
6 I opened to my beloved, but my beloved had turned and
   gone.

  My soul had gone out to him when he spoke.

  I sought him but did not find him;
  I called out to him, but he did not answer me.
7 The watchmen who go about in the city found me.

  They struck me; they bruised me.

  They took my shawl from upon me—those guardians of the
   walls.

---

[10]The word *dôdhîm*, rendered "lovers" here, is argued by some to be rendered "caresses" since that is its meaning elsewhere in the plural in 1:2, 4; 4:10; 7:12. However, its other usages are not precisely parallel for the word has the personal pronoun attached to it in all its other uses. But even if it were identical in form, this verse sets *dôdhîm* parallel to "loved ones," *re'îm*. It is really quite easy to see what the speaker has done. He has made plural the bride's term of address for her husband, *dôdh*, and the husband's frequent term of address for the bride, *ra'yah* and addressed them both in the terms they often called one another.

8   I adjure you, O daughters of Jerusalem,
       if you find my beloved—as to what you will tell him—
       (tell him) that I am faint with love.

Daughters of Jerusalem to Bride

9   What is your beloved more than another lover,
       O fairest among women?
       What is your beloved more than another lover,
       that so you adjure us?

Bride to Daughters of Jerusalem

10   My beloved is dazzlingly ruddy,
       distinguished among ten thousand.

11   His head is pure gold;
       His locks, palm leaves, black as a raven.

12   His eyes are like doves beside streams of water,
       bathed in milk and reposed in their setting.

13   His cheeks are a bed of balsam, a raised bed of spices.
       His lips are lilies, dripping with liquid myrrh.

14   His hands are cylinders of gold set with jewels.
       His abdomen is a plate of ivory covered with sapphires.

15   His legs are alabaster pillars set upon pedestals
       of fine gold.
       His appearance is like Lebanon, choice as the cedars.

16   His mouth is sweetness,
       And all of him is wonderful.
       This is my beloved and this is my friend,
       O daughters of Jerusalem.

Daughters of Jerusalem to Bride

6:1   Where has your beloved gone, O fairest among women?
       Where has your beloved turned, that we may
       seek him with you?

Bride to Daughters of Jerusalem

2   My beloved has gone to his garden, to beds of balsam,

to pasture his flock among the gardens
and to gather lilies.

3   I am my beloved's and my beloved is mine—the one
who pastures his flock among the lilies.

King to Bride

4   Fair you are, my darling, as Tirzah,
lovely as Jerusalem,
awe-inspiring as bannered hosts.

5   (Turn your eyes from me for they arouse me.)[11]
Your hair is like a flock of goats which descend from Gilead.

6   Your teeth are like a flock of young lambs,
which have come up from the washing,
all of which are paired,
and not one among them is alone.

7   Your temples are like a slice of a pomegranate
behind your veil.

8   There are sixty queens and eighty concubines
and maidens without number;

9   (But) unique is she—my dove, my perfect one;
unique is she to her mother;
pure is she to the one who bore her.
The daughters saw her and called her blessed;
The queens and concubines praised her,

10   "Who is this looking forth like the dawn,
fair as the moon,
pure as the sun,
awesome as an army with banners?"

Bride in soliloquy

11   To the garden of nut trees I had gone down
to see the fresh shoots of the ravine,

---

[11]Nahum B. Waldman, "A Note on Canticles 4:9 and 6:15," *Journal of Biblical Literature*, 89 (June, 1970), 216-217.

to see whether the vine had budded or the pomegranates
had bloomed.

12   Before I was aware, my soul set me among the chariots
of my people, a prince.

Daughters of Jerusalem to Bride
13   Return, return O Shulamith;
Return, return, that we may gaze upon you.

King to Daughters of Jerusalem
How you gaze upon Shulamith
as at a dance of Mahanaim![12]

King to Bride
7:2[13] How beautiful are your feet in sandals, O prince's daughter.
The curves of your thighs are like ornaments,
the work of the hands of an artist.

3   Your navel is a rounded goblet never lacking mixed wine.
Your abdomen is a stack of wheat enclosed with lilies.

4   Your two breasts are like two fawns, twins of a gazelle.

5   Your neck is like a tower of ivory.
Your eyes are like the pools in Heshbon
by the gate of the populous city.
Your nose is like a tower in Lebanon keeping watch
over Damascus.

6   Your head crowns you as Carmel,
And the flowing locks of your head are like purple threads.
The king is held captive by your tresses.

---

[12]This translation should be preferred over that of the New American Standard's
"Why should you gaze?" because of the preceding and following context: The
preceding context records in 6:10 the king's observation that the maidens praise
the bride, and this translation continues that observation; in the following context the Hebrew text in both 7:1 (English text, 6:13) and 7:2 (English text, 7:1)
begin with *mah* and seem to be parallel. So they may likely bear the same sense
which is conveyed best by the translation given.
[13]6:13 is 7:1 in the Hebrew text; 7:1 is 7:2 in the Hebrew text and so forth until the end
of this chapter. Chapter eight resumes one to one correspondence.

7   How beautiful and how pleasant you are—love in (your)
     exquisite delights.
8   This your stature is comparable to a palm tree,
         and your breasts to its clusters.
9   I say, "I will climb the palm tree;
     I will take hold of its fruit stalks;
         Oh, may your breasts be like clusters of the vine
             and the fragrance of your breath like apples
10   and your mouth like the best wine..."

Bride (to King)

         ... going down smoothly for my beloved,
             flowing gently through the lips of the sleeping ones.[14]

(in soliloquy)

11   I am my beloved's and his desire is for me.

to King

12   Come, my beloved, let us go out into the country.
     Let us spend the night in the villages.
13   Let us rise early to the vineyards.
     Let us see whether the vine has budded
         and its blossoms have opened
         and whether the pomegranates have bloomed.
     There I will give my caresses to you.
14   The mandrakes have given forth fragrance
         and over our doors are all choice fruits[15]—
             both new and old, which I have stored up for

---

[14]The word *yeshenîm*, rendered "sleeping ones," is the reading of the Massoretic text; the Syriac, Septuagint and Vulgate read very closely *weshinnîm*, "and teeth." The decision for a preferred reading is difficult, but the former can explain the latter and is the more difficult reading. Of course, the *yôdh* may have been confused with the *waw* and unintentionally miscopied.

[15]The word *meghadhîm*, rendered "choice fruits," refers generally to excellent or choice things but always to gifts of nature. The subsequent reference to new and old, that is, newer fresh and older dried fruits, makes it reasonable to identify these particular choice things as fruits.

you, my beloved.

8:1   Oh that you were like a brother to me
who nursed at the breasts of my mother.
If I found you outdoors I would kiss you,
and no one would despise me either.

2   I would lead you;
I would bring you to the house of my mother.
You would instruct me.[16]
I would give you spiced wine to drink, the nectar
of my pomegranate.

3   Oh may his left hand be under my head and his right hand
embrace me.

to Daughters of Jerusalem

4   I adjure you, O daughters of Jerusalem,
not to arouse, not to awaken love until it pleases.

Poet

5   Who is this coming from the wilderness, leaning
on her beloved?

Bride to King

Beneath the apple tree I awakened you;
there your mother was in labor with you;
there she was in labor and gave you birth.

6   Put me as a seal upon your heart,

---

[16]The word *telammedheni*, rendered "you would instruct me," morphologically could be 3 f.s. as well as 2 m.s. In this context it is likely the latter. The bride, having assumed the role of the groom's sister, continues the imaginative wish of 8:1. Were they brother and sister with common mother, she would lead him to their home where he would instruct her. To choose the 3 f.s. reading would be (a) to assume the ellipsis of the relative pronoun and (b) to overlook that the other two verbs address the brother. Zöckler argues further that "a verb thus extraordinarily interrupting this series must necessarily have been indicated not merely by ŝ (which is inserted) or *'asher* but by an emphatic *hî'*; and to this *hî'* would then have to be opposed an *'anî 'ashqeka*." Otto Zöckler, *The Song of Solomon*, trans. by W. Henry Green, *Commentary on the Holy Scriptures*, ed. by John Peter Lange (Grand Rapids: Zondervan Publishing House, 1960), V, p. 121.

As a seal upon your arm.
For strong as death is love.
Relentless as Sheol is jealousy.
Its flashes are flashes of fire,
the flame of Yahweh.

7   Many waters cannot extinguish this love
and rivers will not drown it.
If a man were to give all the possessions of his house
for love, he would be utterly despised.

Brothers of Bride

8   We have a little sister and she has no breasts.
What shall we do for our sister for the day on which
she is spoken for?

9   If she is a wall,
we shall build on her a battlement of silver,
But if she is a door,
we shall enclose her with planks of cedar.

Bride (to all)

10   I was a wall and my breasts were like towers.
Then I became in his eyes as one who finds peace.

11   A vineyard belonged to Solomon at Baal Hamon.
He gave the vineyard to caretakers; each one was to bring
a thousand shekels of silver for its fruit.

12   My own vineyard belongs to me.

to King

The thousand are for you, O Solomon,
and two hundred for the caretakers of the fruit.

King to Bride

13   O you who dwell in the gardens,
(My) companions are listening for your voice.
Let me hear it.

Bride to King
14   Hurry, my beloved,
And be like a gazelle or a young stag
on the mountains of spices.

INTERPRETING
THE
SONG OF SOLOMON

The reader may enjoy *A Song for Lovers* and yet wonder if the interpretation undergirding it is accurate and reliable. Is it not true that the song has been interpreted in many other ways?

The answer is certainly yes, very many other ways. One Old Testament scholar concluded his survey of the various interpretations with this: "Of all the books in the Old Testament none is so difficult to interpret as the Song of Songs. About no other book has so much been written, and concerning no other are there such differences of opinion and such variety of interpretation."[1]

Over five hundred commentaries on the song remain with us from the first seventeen hundred years alone.[2] Yet after these five hundred and perhaps more, the Westminster Assembly observed in 1657 that the commentaries customarily increased the cloud of obscurity they had hoped to remove.[3] Modern commentaries evidently have chosen to continue this same unprofitable tradition. At present among Old Testament scholars no interpretation has had wide acclaim[4] though there has certainly been no lack of acclaimed interpreters.

Some of these will still maintain one of several allegorical views; others, a literal two- or three-character dramatic view; still others, that the song is the liturgy for a fertility cult. For a while the song was popularly conceived as a collection of songs for a wedding feast; and many, especially today, maintain that it is only an anthology of disconnected love poems. The Song of Songs has indeed been interpreted in other ways.

But should not the real question be, "Has it been interpreted accurately in other ways?" In order to answer this question I wrote a thesis evaluating the other interpretations and setting forth the reasons for my own.[5] Without going into tiresome technical detail, I would like to present the more important conclusions reached in that thesis.

This appendix, therefore, first describes and evaluates each of the major interpretations which have been given to the Song of Solomon. Then it sets forth the interpretation upon which the present book is based. In explaining this interpretation, I will first articulate the interpretive method and then explain the results which logically unfold from the application of that method.

The Allegorical Interpretation

The oldest interpretation in print is the one regarding the song as an allegory. Almost all interpreters until the Reformation interpreted the song in this way.[6] The Jewish interpreters discovered an allegory of God and Israel. The Christian interpreters discovered an allegory of Christ and the Church. A few relatively recent allegorists discovered a pagan allegory of the gods Baal and Astarte.[7] Within this threefold framework one may further subdivide each category into almost as many interpretations as there are interpreters. For although the allegorical interpreters are often in a general agreement on the fundamental characters, they differ widely on their interpretation of detail.

This multiplicity of interpretations constitutes one reason why the allegorical interpretation has now been almost completely abandoned. For unless a literary work is an allegory, the allegorical method of interpreting it normally yields a host of divergent interpretations. An intelligible allegory, on the other hand, will usually guide the reader to its intended interpretation with special signposts along the way. For example, the names of Christian, Hopeful or Worldly-Wiseman in Bunyan's *Pilgrims Progress* clearly reveal whom they represent. Now, of course, it is not always that easy. But the fact that with the Song of Solomon the allegorists never agree, or even show with some degree of plausibility, why one allegorical version should be preferred over another has raised a proper suspicion that the song should never have been regarded as an allegory in the first place.

Other considerations confirm that suspicion. For one, when the man-woman relationship is occasionally used symbolically in the Old Testament, it is always accompanied by an explicit indication, as, for example, in Ezekiel 16:3 or Hosea 1—3.

Furthermore, neither the author nor the character of the work lead one to suspect an allegory. The poet Herder observed this when he wrote, "When I read the book itself I do not find the slightest intimation or even the faintest trace that such a sense was the design of the author. . . . In the life of Solomon I discover still less reason for this concealed sense, be it historical, mystical, metaphysical, or political. For Solomon's wisdom did not consist in mysticism, much less in metaphysics, or scholastic church history. His wisdom was displayed in his common sense, as seen in his view of the things of this life."[8]

The burden of proof is surely on the one hand claiming the song to be an allegory. Still one may wonder why it achieved such popularity for so long in Western history. The answer probably lies in the sexual attitudes held by the interpreters in that particular time.

The Medieval Age is famous for the asceticism of its religious world—the very world from which came the interpreters of the song, of course. And these men frequently assumed a Platonic dualism of spirit and matter or of mind and body. This in turn led to a rejection of the goodness of the body and a disapproval of the sexual expression of love even in marriage. No less a theologian than Augustine fell into this error, genuinely espousing the view that the only purpose for intercourse is the bearing of children and that before the fall of Adam it was not necessary even for that.

Sex was clearly regarded as a necessary evil in the medieval world. It is therefore not unexpected that a song celebrating the goodness of marital love was allegorized to celebrate something less offensive. Nevertheless, the modern world with its sexual frankness can scarcely feel the weight of this medieval argument and that, combined with the other intrinsic weaknesses of the allegorical interpretation, must lead to its rejection.

The Syrian Wedding Feast Interpretation

Another major theory which rose in its place was the Syrian wedding feast view or epithalamic theory. Certain early scholars such as Lightfoot, Lowth and Percy understood the song as a single epithalamium in honor of Solomon's marriage to Pharaoh's daughter. This was later developed and transformed by J. S. Wetzstein and then elaborated upon by Budde and adopted by Bewer, Cassuto, Cornill, Goodspeed, M. Jastrow, Riehm, Siegfried and others.

This interpretation regards the song as a collection of wedding songs from a seven-day Jewish marriage festival like the Syrian one. The proponents of this theory admit that a seven-day wedding feast is not explicitly taught as the background of the Song of Solomon. Nevertheless, they affirm that such a background must be inferred because of numerous parallels between the event described in the song and the events of the seven-day Syrian marriage feast. The following similarities of the song and Syrian practice have been alleged as reasons.

Both portray the bride and groom as king and queen. Both occur in spring. Both crown the bride and groom. Both center around a feast, for in 5:1 the wedding guests are invited to eat the refreshments. Both contain the praise songs (called *wasfs*) of the bride and groom. Both reveal the bride performing a sword dance on her wedding day. And, finally, both fetch the bride in a litter.

It seems doubtful, however, that these reasons can sustain the wedding feast view, for it is perhaps trivial that both occur in spring and both contain *wasf*-like songs. Spring is a universal time for love and marriage—common to romantic literature of every age. And the *wasf*-like praise songs are found in Egyptian love songs, where there is no evidence whatsoever of any seven-day feast.[9]

But more importantly, it is untrue that both portray the bride and groom as king and queen who furthermore are both crowned; for Shulamith is never given the title of queen, and it is the king, not she, who is crowned (3:11). Yet in the Syrian custom only the bride is crowned. It is also doubtful that both fetch the bride in a litter, for even though the bride may possibly be in the procession of 3:6-11, the king is the actual focus and the text does not indicate he has fetched his bride. Furthermore, to adduce 5:1 ("Eat, O loved ones; drink and be drunk, O lovers") as evidence of a literal feast is to misunderstand that verse and its context. For the speaker is addressing the lovers and not their wedding guests.

Finally, to interpret 7:2-8 as a description of a sword dance by the bride is preposterous. The words do not describe a dance[10] but instead describe his lovely wife before they make love—as the context clearly informs us (7:9-10). So the alleged parallels to the Syrian customs thoroughly break down. And with the collapse of the alleged parallels must come the collapse of the theory resting upon them.

The Three-Character Dramatic Interpretation

Another major interpretation to take center stage was the three-character dramatic view. This interpretation maintains that the story of the song centers around the theme of Shulamith's faithfulness to her beloved shepherd in spite of King Solomon's advances. The earliest proponent of three characters was Ibn Ezra in the twelfth century A.D., although he still interpreted the song allegorically. But the first Jewish exegete to maintain both a literal and a three-character view was S. Lowisohn in 1816. The first Christian scholar to develop this was Jacobi in 1771. In 1826 Ewald developed the theory. Its adoption in 1891 by Driver in his introduction to the Old Testament popularized it.[11]

The four strongest arguments for this interpretation are as follows: (1) Solomon would not likely appear as a shepherd as in 1:7 and 6:2;[12] (2) Solomon's infamous reputation as a lover would preclude his being the participant in the preeminently exemplary romance of the Scriptures; even within the song he refers to his harem (6:8);[13] (3) The moral of the poem in 8:7b, "If a man were to give all the possessions of his house for love he would be utterly despised," is more compatible with the resistance of Shulamith to Solomon's pomp and wealth;[14] and (4) Solomon's speeches are vulgar and "frigid flatteries... descriptions of physical beauty with no thought of moral qualities... (which likely) have done duty before" (1:9-11; 4:1-7; 6:4-10; 7:2-10), whereas the bride's speech is a reflection of a pure and genuine love (4:8-15).[15]

These are the pillars of support for the three-character dramatic view. But perhaps the following considerations will dislodge them.

1. *The Shepherd Role.* It is false historically and literarily that Solomon could not assume the role of a shepherd. Historically it is false because Solomon did have many flocks and herds (Eccles. 2:7). And it was not a title of disrespect, for even the Messiah was conceived as the ideal shepherd of the flock of Israel (Ezek. 34:1-24).

Literarily it is false because of internal and external evidence for "role playing" among lovers. Within the Song itself the bride is portrayed as a humble maiden (1:6) and a princess (7:2), and she longs to be as a sister (8:1) and even a seal (8:6). The husband is not only king (3:7, 9, 11) but also a shepherd (1:7-8) and brother (8:1). The external evidence for role playing comes from the Egyptian love songs which are the closest literary parallels to Canticles in the ancient world. In the process of tabulating some of these parallels Rylaardsdam observes that,

> There are . . . special literary forms that are conspicuous in both the Egyptian lyrics and the Song. The first of these is "travesty." This is a role playing device. To facilitate their desire to be near each other the lovers impersonate characters or relationships which, in fantasy, effect their desire. The travesty appears to be a prominent feature in the Song also and to provide the clue to some once baffling passages, e.g., 1:5-7 . . . [where] her lover plays the role of a shepherd. [16]

Nevertheless, one must be careful not to assign all "roles" to fantasy, for the husband is genuinely portrayed as King Solomon; and the bride, in light of the narrative of 1:5-7, which seems to be further explained in 8:10-12, was evidently indeed a humble maiden lifted to royalty.

2. *Solomon's Promiscuity.* If Canticles is a literary fiction designed simply to instruct about marriage, this objection loses its force. For the wisdom of Solomon's proverbs is not abrogated by his unwise behavior, nor are the psalms of David deprived of any value because of his escapade with Bathsheba. But if Canticles is not a fiction, it is still not absolutely incumbent upon the interpreter to explain how a promiscuous man could at one time in his life experience genuine marital love. Nonetheless, one may speculate.

This was probably written early in Solomon's life. The presence of so small a harem would indicate this, for later it totalled not 140 (6:8) but a thousand (1 Kings 11:3). The problem raised by the presence of a harem of any size, however, may be explained in one of three ways. First, it may actually have been the possession of Solomon which he enjoyed until he was lifted from it to the pure love of Canticles. Or second, it was perhaps an inheritance from his father David,[17] for we are not told how many wives and concubines David added the last twenty years of his life; and if Solomon could add 860 in his reign, David could have added a hundred in his. Yet once having received this inheritance, we might imagine Solomon not indulging in its enjoyment. Or third, we might reject the latter two views and assign the "sixty queens" of 6:8 to the sixty mighty men of the marriage procession (3:7) who would also own the concubines, for only here in the entire Old Testament is the feminine of *melek* used to refer to the king's wives. Elsewhere it refers to foreign queens,[18] so perhaps here it merely refers to the wives of the nobility as royalty. The queens do seem to be set parallel to the daughters of Jerusalem in 6:9. "The daughters saw her and called her blessed, the queens and concubines praised her." If these are truly parallel then it should be observed that the daughters of Jerusalem are not represented in the Song as wives but as royalty ready to do the king's bidding. And furthermore, it should be noted that the king does not claim the possession of sixty queens and eighty concubines, but merely the existence of them, and that in order to contrast them to his wife: "There are sixty queens and eighty concubines, and maidens without number, but unique is she—my dove, my perfect one."

At any rate, each view supposes the events of Canticles to be early and this supposition is supported by the small size of the harem whether it belonged to Solomon or others. But dating romance early in Solomon's reign makes eminently good psychological sense as well. For in the light of his other writings one might

agree with the rabbi who placed the Song early by observing that
"when a man is young, he sings songs. When he becomes an adult,
he utters practical proverbs. When he becomes old, he voices the
vanity of things."[19] And more seriously with respect to the psychological sense, one might imagine that so lofty a love as Canticles
depicts, if taken away by death, might effect an empty and fruit-
less search to replace it with the many wives Solomon later possessed. His writing of wise proverbs did not later prevent his unwise behavior. So perhaps it is only consistent with the character
of Solomon that the faithful love of Canticles would not prevent his
later promiscuous affairs. Solomon was that kind of a man.

3. *The Moral of the Poem.* The so-called moral of the poem is not
merely 8:7b; rather the climax of the song is all of 8:5-7 where love is
extolled for its strength and fierce possession of the person loved.
And this, in fact, is a perfect commentary on the love relationship
which blossoms in Canticles. For here the woman finds greater
security and more open response as the relationship progresses.
This progression is traced throughout the thesis. The addition of
8:7b, as the reader shall see, serves as a fine transition from the
recent acknowledgment that their love is a gift from God in 8:6 to
the resolution of 8:8-14 wherein it is seen that God freely gave this
gift through providence (8:8-9), and now the woman would freely
give herself to Solomon (8:10-12).

4. *Solomon's Speeches.* Solomon's speeches are supposedly set
in contrast to "the beloved's" speech of 4:8-15. Yet surely his physical description of her in 4:1-7 is no more sensual than the beloved's
description of her caresses (*dôdhîm* in 4:10) and kisses (4:11). And
Solomon's "speeches" are obviously well received by the bride, for
following what is supposedly the crassest of his praises in 7:2-10
the bride continues the imagery of her kisses like wine by respond-
ing that the wine "goes down smoothly for her beloved, flowing
gently through the lips of the sleeping ones." So she falls asleep in

his arms echoing his very words. The *coup de grace* to this fourth pillar, however, must come from the plain fact that the bride reciprocates her beloved king's praises in precisely the same kind of terms in which they were given (5:10-16). Solomon's endearing praises of his wife may be too coarse for some interpreters, but they were not so for his wife.

The Modern Anthologist Interpretation

So the three-character dramatic view, like the previous interpretations, also fails to display adequate foundation. In light of its failure and the failures of its predecessors, the majority of modern interpreters have concluded that the song is a mere collection of disconnected poems about love which "teaches no lesson and tells no story."[20] Scholars holding this view include Baudissin, Bettan, Bleek, Castelli, DeWette, Dopke, Eichhorn, Eissfeldt, Gordis, Graetz, Haupt, Jakob, Kleuker, Landsberger, Lods, Loisy, Magnus, Margoliouth, Meier, Noyes, Oesterloy, Reuss, Robinson, Rowley, Simon, Staerk, Young and Zunz.

Nevertheless, the song does claim to be a single song and not a collection. It claims a unity of meaning for itself. But in the final analysis the modern position is the only tenable one unless such a unity of meaning can be displayed.

A New Interpretation

It was just such a unity of meaning I attempted to display in my thesis. I did so by employing the following hermeneutical method. First the book was carefully translated from its original language. Then the identities of the speakers were ascertained. Although this occasionally appears difficult in the English text, the Hebrew language makes this easier because it contains a masculine and feminine "you." So, for example, when one speaker addressed a feminine "you," Solomon was the likely speaker. More importantly, it became clear as I read the song that each lover normally addresses the other with a characteristic term of affection. This also reveals the speaker.

All this made identification easy. But the rest was like putting together a jigsaw puzzle. The best way to put together a jigsaw puzzle is first to join the boundary pieces. They are easily recognized because they have a straight side. But then the second step is to piece together the most easily distinguishable objects as, for example, a person or a house. This is much easier than joining together unnecessarily related detail.

This very same procedure was adopted in interpreting the Song of Songs. First, the most obvious boundaries clearly demarcated by a change of scene, speaker or refrain were observed. For instance, not a single interpreter doubts the boundaries of the wedding procession in 3:6-11. Almost equally as obvious are the lovemaking sections of 4:1—5:1 and 7:2-10. After the meanings of each of these fundamental sections were determined and an apparent pattern was beginning to crystallize, the remaining sections of the poem were analyzed as well.

Although they are admittedly more difficult, at last they too were solved and all the sections of the puzzle could be pieced together. The story had crystallized, and the picture of the couple's romance was clearly visible.

As an example of the analysis already referred to, consider the boundaried segment of 4:1—5:1. The pieces of that section of the puzzle include a praise section (4:1-7), a call from afar (4:8), evident caresses (4:9-11), extended metaphor of a garden and spring (4:12—5:1), a new term of address (bride), an indication she was wearing a veil (4:1, 3), a more delicate atmosphere than the other lovemaking section (comparing 4:12—5:1 with 7:2-10), as well as a less sensuous description of praise, and lastly its sequence in following the wedding procession of 3:6-11.

It seemed quite certain that in the lovely imagery of garden and spring their love is consummated. And it followed that 4:9-11 expresses the lovemaking that preceded it. The opening praise section then was logically and psychologically explained as the beginning of their time together. This supposition found confirmation in 7:2-10 where it is clear that the praise immediately precedes their lovemaking. The only verse left to integrate was 4:8, and it did seem necessary to integrate it or else 4:9 would be an unprecedentedly and unrepeatedly abrupt entrance to their intimacies. In light of the royal wedding psalm's single command for the bride to mentally leave her homeland,[21] the psychological possibility of insecurity on a wedding night, and the certain indication that the request was metaphorical, it was natural to interpret it as a summons to draw her fearful thoughts to her loving husband.

So a unified lovemaking sequence could be established. But was it a wedding night? The other pieces of the puzzle answered yes. For the first time she was called a bride. She wore a veil, a custom only for the wedding night. The delicate atmosphere confirmed it, and, of course, it followed the wedding procession.

In less detail here is a brief summary of the inductive sequence of thought leading to the interpretation of the entire book. After interpreting the wedding procession and lovemaking sections (3:6-11; 4:1—5:1 and 7:2-10 with its corollary of 7:11—8:3) I examined the conflict and solution section (5:2—6:13). Although problems of detail were painstakingly and meticulously examined in the thesis, the essential breakdown of this section can be seen in a glance. Its constituent sections were distinguished both structurally and logically: structurally, 5:2-8 portrayed the problem of ingratitude; then logically, four questions mark the progression of thought —5:9; 6:1; 6:10 and 6:12. The first question signals her realization of gratitude for her husband. The second initiates her seeking him and being praised by him (forgiveness). The third reveals her reunion with him, and the fourth closes the section with either a dismissal of any third party or a notice that all seek to behold Shulamith. On either view of the final question, it serves as a fine transition to her husband's unique privilege of beholding his wife as they make love.

The next section analyzed was 1:1—3:5, later discovered to be the courtship account. Its opening subsections were very brief (1:1-4a, 4b-8, 9-11), but their content was expanded and developed in 1:12-14; 1:15—2:6; 2:8-14; 2:15-17 and 3:1-4. In studying the latter subsections I found, fortunately, that a pattern developed around the twice repeated refrain of 2:7 and 3:5. The two contexts of that refrain followed the pattern of "longing" (2:6 and 3:1-4), appeal for patience (2:7 and 3:5) and reward of progress in their relationship (2:8-14 and 3:6-11). And quite significantly the second pattern was more intense, a confirmation that we were reading the development of a courtship. It was then no problem to review the initially brief sections which began the song. They were thematic, introducing portraits of each lover and the beginnings of mutual appreciation.

Further confirmation that 1:1—3:5 was indeed purely a courtship section and not, say, reflections on married life could be seen in a variety of ways. First, the movement from 4:1 to the climax of 8:5-7 is clearly intended to be one of chronological progression. The only flashback is in the resolution of 8:8-14 where it would be expected. One must recall, for example, that a comparison of the lovemaking sections of chapters four and seven revealed a progression in intimacy and frankness. Also, even within the courtship section, there is movement in intensity until the wedding day. Furthermore, although there is longing for the physical expression of love, there is no fulfillment until the wedding night. The request of Shulamith for such fulfillment (2:17), for example, is not granted until the wedding night (4:6). Surely Schonfield is right when he concludes:

> The first half [the first section of 1:1–3:5] reflected a mood of expectation. The bride-to-be is waiting for her beloved, longing for him, excusing her own defects, fancying she hears him calling, fearing that perhaps she has lost him. Finally, the groom is seen coming with his escort. . . . The mood of the next part is one of fulfillment, for the wedding days are here and the girl is addressed as "my bride." [22]

The last section analyzed was 8:5-14, which revealed itself to be the climax and resolution of the song. Most interpreters agree that if there is a climax to the song, it is definitely in 8:5-7. The resolution, however, is more difficult to locate. Still, the last words of the climax do implicitly raise the question of how such a love can be gained. A careful analysis shows that the resolution, particularly coupled with the information from 1:6, answers that question. Love cannot be bought, but it can be given by God through providence (8:8-9) working through personal responsibility (8:10) which culminates in the giving of the one person to the other (8:11-12). The last two verses, in re-echoing earlier words of the couple, function like a coda in a symphony and emphasize the dynamic rather than static quality of their love.

Having discovered the meaning of the six major sections now, it became obvious that the development of their love story was as harmoniously unfolded as a symphony. One can remember the opening thematic sections which function like introductory themes in a sonata-allegro symphony. Thematic development follows, ultimately reaching a climax and resolution. Thus the refrains that occur within the song are like the transitions or bridges of a symphony. Both may have separate and important themes. Moreover, as the symphony's final notes frequently recall thematic elements from previous sections, so does the ending of our song.

Needless to say, the author of our song did not originate the aes-

INTERPRETING THE SONG OF SOLOMON

thetic medium of the classical symphony, but the happy analogy to it does reveal the remarkably precise unity of his work. The form was perfectly wed to the content. The poet was a composer who displayed a beautiful romance in exquisite symphonic form!

Notes

[1]Theophile J. Meek, Hugh Thompson Kerr, Jr., "The Song of Songs," *The Interpreter's Bible*, ed. Nolan B. Harmon (New York: Abingdon, 1939), V, p. 91.

[2]George Louis Scheper, "The Spiritual Marriage: The Exegetic History and Literary Impact of the Song of Songs in the Middle Ages," Diss. Princeton 1971, p. 10.

[3]Ibid., p. 5.

[4]Robert B. Dempsey, "The Interpretation and Use of the Song of Songs," Diss. Boston University School of Theology 1963, p. 97. Summaries of the history of its interpretation may be found in Scheper's work in its entirety; Dempsey, pp. 57-95; Robert Pfeiffer, *An Introduction to the Books of the Old Testament* (New York: Harper and Brothers, 1941), pp. 714-716; and more recently, G. Fohrer and E. Sellin, *Introduction to the Old Testament*, trans. D. E. Green (New York: Abingdon, 1968).

[5]S. Craig Glickman, "The Unity of the Song of Solomon," Thesis Dallas Theological Seminary 1974.

[6]Scheper, "The Spiritual Marriage," Bruce Waltke, "Canticles," unpublished article for the new edition of the *International Standard Bible Encyclopedia*. For the pagan allegory version see Theophile J. Meek, "The Song of Songs and the Fertility Cult," *The Song of Songs, a Symposium*, ed. Wildfred H. Schoff (Philadelphia: The Commercial Museum, 1924), p. 48.

[7]For a more complete and helpful analysis of the cultic allegory refer to Arthur Farstad, "Literary Genre of the Song of Songs," Thesis Dallas Theological Seminary 1967, pp. 48-60. For further description and refutation see also H. H. Rowley, *The Servant of the Lord and Other Essays* (London: Lutterworth, 1952), pp. 230-242.

[8]Waltke, "Canticles."

[9]William Kelly Simpson, *The Literature of Ancient Egypt* (New Haven: Yale, 1972), p. 316.

[10]Glickman, "The Unity of the Song of Solomon," pp. 58-60.

[11]Christian D. Ginsburg, *The Song of Songs and Coheleth* (New York: KTVA, 1970) contains an excellent summary as does Rowley, *Servant of the Lord.*

[12]S. R. Driver, *An Introduction to the Literature of the Old Testament* (New York: Charles Scribners Sons, 1891), p. 417 and F. Godet, "The Interpretation of the Song of Songs," *Classical Evangelical Essays in Old Testament Interpretation*, ed. Walter C. Kaiser, Jr. (Grand Rapids: Baker, 1972), p. 152.

[13]Driver, *Introduction*, p. 417; Gleason L. Archer, Jr., *A Survey of Old Testament Introduction* (Chicago: Moody, 1964), p. 476.

[14]Godet, "The Interpretation of the Song of Songs," p. 152.

[15]William Walter Cannon, *The Song of Songs* (Cambridge: University Press, 1913), p. 17.

[16]J. Coert Rylaardsdam, "The Song of Songs and Biblical Faith," *Biblical Research*, 10 (1965), p. 13; G. Fohrer and E. Sellin, *Introduction to the Old Testament*, trans. D. E. Green (New York: Abingdon, 1968), p. 302.

[17]Roland de Vaux, *Ancient Israel* (New York: McGraw-Hill, 1965), p. 116. He cites several passages in which "it appears that the king's harem, at least in the early days of the monarchy, used to pass to his successor."

[18]Ibid., p. 117.

[19]Midrash Shir Hashirim Rabba 1.1 as quoted by Robert Gordis, *The Song of Songs* (New York: The Jewish Theological Seminary, 1954), p. 56.

[20]N. H. Gottwald, "The Song of Songs," *Interpreters Dictionary of the Bible*, ed. George Arthur Buttrick (New York: Abingdon, 1962), IV, p. 424.

[21]Listen, O daughter, give attention and incline your ear;

Forget your people and your father's house;

Then the King will desire your beauty.   *Psalm 45:10-11a, NASV*

[22]Hugh J. Schonfield, *The Song of Songs* (New York: Mentor, 1959), p. 106.